Will You Take This Woman?

A Play in Two Acts

by

MAURICE CALLARD

NEW PLAYWRIGHTS NETWORK,
35, SANDRINGHAM ROAD,
MACCLESFIELD,
CHESHIRE SK10 1QB

First Published March 1974

490076181

Printed in Great Britain by
Ambassador Press Ltd., Macclesfield, Cheshire.

PRODUCTION NOTES

It cannot be stressed too strongly that farce should always be played 'straight', that is to say, the actor should not doubt the genuineness of the character he is playing. Herbert, for instance, is a brash, ignorant boor but he is the sort of man who believes that he, and he alone, is right about everything. In his own regard, he is the most sincere man on earth, and he should be played as if he believed in himself and everything he does.

So with all the other characters, and producers would do well to scotch any attempts of players to 'do funny things to try and get laughs'.

As a general rule in farce, where laughs depend on action, the play should proceed through the laughter. Where it depends on words, the actors will have to time their speeches so that dialogue is not lost. There is less visual funniness in this play than in many farces. The laughs will arise from the incongruousness of the situations and particularly from the inappropriateness of the language in a particular context. A very great number of the lines can be expected to get a laugh, and very often one laugh line is followed immediately by another. Timing, therefore, becomes of supreme importance.

In a general sense, this is an easy play to stage . . . there are no chases, no disguises, no dashing in and out of bedroom doors. The set is simple but a producer might like it to reflect the temperaments of the occupants . . . the loud Herbert who has been on the 'fiddle' all his life on the one hand and the ineffectual Pauline who was once on the stage and is still a bit arty. A parody of good taste would be appropriate.

All the parts should be played with a verve and gusto. The half-hearted . . . the subtle, even . . . has no place in this sort of romp.

The two characters who come nearest to being 'straight' are Jenny and Derek. Jenny is starry-eyed and should give the impression that she is infatuated with Derek. He is unaware of this and his lines (in scenes with her) have a double entendre. He is business-like, obsessed with his film-making, She is able to interpret his speeches to her quite differently.

A good wedding cake can be made from polystyrene and a 'trick' knife from a genuine handle into which is fitted a cardboard blade smoothly covered with Bacofoil. For those not old enough to remember, a Carmen Miranda hat is large and decorated with masses of bright fruits. At the beginning of the final scene it should be remembered that all the guests we do not see are in the marquee in the garden. Their presence should be made known to the audience from occasional ribald screams and guffaws of laughter.

Have fun !

CHARACTERS

PAULINE FARSON — Middle Aged
HERBERT FARSON — Parents of Jenny and Fiona

JENNY FARSON — (17)

FIONA FARSON — (28-30)

THE VICAR

GERALD DUNJON — (23)

DEREK COLBERT — (25)

AUNT MELINDA — Middle Age

IVY DUNJON — Middle Aged - Parents of Gerald.
RONALD DUNJON —

JOHNNY SPINET — (30)

The action of the play takes place in the living-room of the Farsons' house in a South-coast town. It is a very warm period in early August.

ACT ONE.   Scene 1.   Early evening.
            Scene 2.   Later in the same evening.

ACT TWO.   Scene 1.   Some days later, about 11 a.m.
            Scene 2.   That afternoon.
            Scene 3.   A couple of hours later.

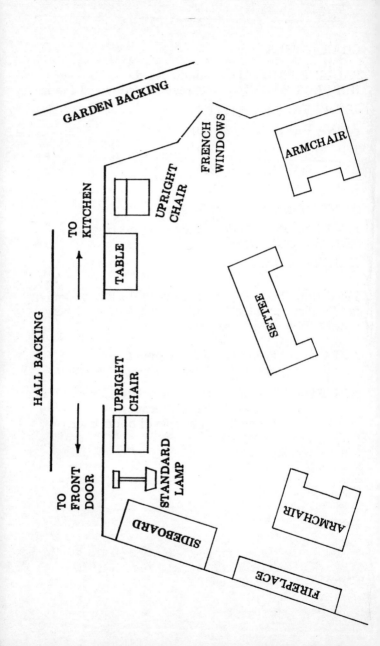

WILL YOU TAKE THIS WOMAN?

ACT ONE

Scene One. The Farson's Living-room. It is the early evening of a warm summer day.
HERBERT FARSON comes in from the garden through the french windows L. carrying a bunch of fresh-cut roses which he takes out to kitchen. After a moment he returns to the garden. He is singing all the time.
PAULINE FARSON comes from kitchen, singing, collects a rose bowl from the room and returns to kitchen.
JENNY FARSON comes downstairs and into room, singing. She stands in front of the mirror above sideboard R. spraying her hair with lacquer from an aerosol.
PAULINE enters with filled rose bowl which she places on table U.C. She is still singing but stops when she realises JENNY is in the room.

PAULINE. That's not my Mum, is it?

JENNY. Gosh, I hope not.*(She looks at aerosol, sighs with relief.)* It's all right. It's hair lacquer.

PAULINE. You be careful with it, then. When you look in the bathroom mirror it's like peering through a blizzard.

JENNY. That'll be Fiona. Her hand shakes. Nerves, you know.

PAULINE. *(As she arranges the roses)* Aren't they lovely? Your father's so proud of his 'Chastity' this year.

JENNY. So am I. *(Turning to PAULINE)* How do I look?

PAULINE. Goodness, gracious.

JENNY. Not too glam, is it?

PAULINE. You have laid it on a bit.

JENNY. Like the eyelashes?

PAULINE. Darling, remember you're still a schoolgirl.

JENNY. No I'm not. I left yesterday.

PAULINE. But you're going back next term to take your A-levels. You're the only clever one in the family and we don't want you wasted.

JENNY. I doubt if I'll go back. I might have a career by then?

PAULINE. *(Worried)* Career?

JENNY. Yes, I mean a career like father . . . well, like most men have.

PAULINE. But you're not trained.

JENNY. *(Indicating that she thinks she's attractive)* I have assets.

PAULINE. (*moving L. anxiously and glancing out into garden*) Don't let your father hear you say such things.

JENNY. I don't want him to know until it's all fixed up.

PAULINE. *(Still worried)* What's going to be fixed up?

JENNY. A part in a film. *(Pause)* Now don't look so doubtful. You were on the stage once remember.

PAULINE. *(Firmly)* The stage is different. Everyone is devoted to his art in the theatre. In films they're devoted to one another. And films attract a very peculiar type of man ... because ... because ... well, there's more money in films.

JENNY. This isn't an ordinary film.

PAULINE. Oh, God, no! Not one of those for men only.

JENNY. No, It's for television. One of those intellectual things they put on late on Sunday evenings when all the working-class people are in bed.

PAULINE. I never watch those. I'm always in bed.

JENNY. Derek is working on one on the life of Modigliani. He was an artist. Painted all his faces about two inches wide and about four foot long. The critics said he was a genius with an individual insight. But he was only painting what he saw. There was something very wrong with his eyes.

PAULINE. And who is Derek?

JENNY. Oh, mother, if you've any aspirations towards culture you must have heard of him. Derek Colbert. He'll soon be as famous as Ken Russell, you see if he's not.

PAULINE. *(Alarmed)* Ken Russell? you mean that young man over in No. 17 who's changed his sex ... twice?

JENNY. *(Brusquely)* No. This one can make up his mind.

PAULINE. But darling, what do you know about acting?

JENNY. *(Buttering her up)* I must have inherited some of your talent, dear.

PAULINE. *(Preening herself)* I do hope you have. It's a wonderful thing ... to have the talent I had.

JENNY. In any case, I've only got to look the part. Derek says he'll tell me what to do. Sheer luck meeting him. He's down here for Cowes and he's got his yacht in the marina. Our chairman managed to get him to give a talk to our cine club. He came up to me afterwards and asked me if I was interested. *(PAULINE looks aghast.)* I mean, interested in taking a part in a film.

PAULINE. Oh, darling, I'm worried. He must be years older than you.

JENNY. If he was younger he'd be the only child film director in the world. Oh, don't look so glum, mum. This is my great chance.

PAULINE. I only know that if any harm comes to you your father will flay this Derek alive. We've had enough trouble over the years with Fiona.

JENNY. Look, mother, I'm not an innocent baby. I can tell you we've had biology lessons at school that'd make your hair curl.

PAULINE. Biology may be all right for telling you what happens but it's not much good for making sure that what happens doesn't happen.

FIONA Farson enters, She is in a temper.

FIONA. *(To JENNY)* You little beast. You've got my lacquer.

JENNY. Yours? Oh, I'm sorry.

FIONA. You know it's mine. You never buy any.

JENNY. Surely you can spare a couple of quick squirts.

FIONA. *(Grabbing the tin)* It's empty. You rotten little thief. *(She makes to muss Jenny's hair.)*

JENNY. *(Jumping back)* Don't touch my hair.

FIONA. Oh, mother, her hair's so stiff you'd cut your hands to ribbons on it.

PAULINE. Don't make a fuss, Fiona. You can use mine.

FIONA. There isn't any of yours left. I used it yesterday

JENNY. It's rotten lacquer, anyway.

FIONA. *(Crying with anger and frustration)* Oh, mother she's got my eyelashes, too.

JENNY. You can have them back tomorrow. I need the tonight.

FIONA. What are you going to say to her, mother? Dressed up like a film star.

PAULINE. Can't you take a little bit off, dear?

JENNY. No. That would smudge the whole effect.

FIONA. You look cheap..

JENNY. *(Moving U.L.)* That's because it's cheap lacquer Tell, Dad, I've gone to a meeting of the cine club.

PAULINE. Have you got your key? We might trot over to Aunt Melinda's. In that case we won't be back until eleven.

JENNY. Eleven suits me fine.

PAULINE. *(Laying down the law)* You're to be in at ten I put you on your honour.

FIONA. *(Who can't see why JENNY should be trusted)* Honour! Ugh!

JENNY. Okay, ten. Means I'll have to cram more into the evening, that's all. Bye, bye. *(She goes out. We hear the front door noisily shut.)*

FIONA. *(In a temper)* She's going out with a man, isn't she?

PAULINE. No, dear. Not a man. A film director.

FIONA. I'm going to tell Dad.

PAULINE. *(Moving to cut off FIONA.s advance to french windows)* No, don't please. He'd go mad if he knew.

FIONA. *(Calmer, moving to look out french windows.)* What's he doing out there, anyway?

PAULINE. *(Turning her head towards C.)* Pruning the roses.

FIONA. On his knees? Peeping through that gap in the fence?

PAULINE. *(Turning from windows in disgust)* O, I don't know! Men! They've always got one thing on their mind. Gerald's the same. When I first met him at Chris's party I thought, Here's a shy little fellow! But in the taxi when he was bringing me home it was like wrestling with an octopus.

PAULINE. Well, make sure you hold him at bay till you're married. I've always thought you gave in too easily in the past.

FIONA. What do you mean? Gave in too easily.

PAULINE. Your attitudes been too eager. Men like women to be aloof, superior. Then, finally, when they get them they imagine they've achieved the impossible ... and that keeps them happy for years.

FIONA. I don't have to worry about Gerald. I think he really wants to get married. Good Lord, look at Dad now. He'll be in next door in a minute.

PAULINE. *(Crosses to window.)* He's gone far enough. *(Calling)* Herbert! Herbert, I want you.

FIONA. *(Crossing and looking in mirror R.)* Oh, look at my hair. Unless I gum it into place it slips all over the show.

PAULINE. The hair is a mystery.

FIONA. Eh?

PAULINE. The hair is a mystery. I had to say that once.

FIONA. Whatever for?

PAULINE. It was in a play I was in.

FIONA. Oh!

HERBERT Farson enters from garden.

HERBERT. What do you want?

PAULINE. I want you to come away from that fence, Herbert.

HERBERT. I was mending it. There's a great gap in it.

PAULINE. Yes, I know. And you made it.

HERBERT. What are you on about?

PAULINE. Mrs. Tovey's lying out there on her lawn in her scarlet bikini, isn't she?

HERBERT. *(Innocently)* How would I know? I've bee busy.

PAULINE. I know you hate gardening and these hot summer evenings you spend in the garden always en at that and where the gap is.

HERBERT. *(Hurt)* I've been pruning the roses.

PAULINE. Oh, yes, when I've been looking you've bee pruning the roses but when you think I haven't bee looking you've been looking ... at Mata Hari next do

HERBERT. How do you know what I'm looking at wh you're not looking at me?

PAULINE. I can tell. You've got a guilty look in your eyes.

FIONA. That's not a guilty look. That's eye-strain.

HERBERT. I'll ask you to show a bit more respect, yo lady,

FIONA. Mother's right. You've got the makings of a d old man, pop.

PAULINE. How dare you speak to your father like tha Pop, indeed!

HERBERT. Anyway, it's a silly argument. Anyone wit grain of sense would know you'd get a much better view from the back bedroom.

FIONA. Oh! Is that why I found your binoculars on th sill?

HERBERT. I was bird watching.

PAULINE. Well, don't watch that bird.

HERBERT. I've had enough of this pettiness. I'm going back to finish my roses. *(Takes his handkerchief from his pocket.)* But just to put your mind at rest, Pauline, I'll wear a blindfold. *(Ties handkerchief around his eyes as he moves towards french windows.)*

PAULINE. It'll give your eyes a rest, anyway.

HERBERT stomps off with a growl of Disgust.

PAULINE. Why were you so rude to your father, Fiona? Calling him a dirty old man.

FIONA. Well, he is.

PAULINE . You know that and I know it. And he knows it. But he ought not to be told. All my life I've had to keep the peace between you girls and your father.

FIONA. Oh, don't be so dramatic, mother. Keep the peace There's been a row in this house as far back as I can remember.

PAULINE. But I've always managed to keep him from striking you. You must admit that. Well, that's what I mean by keeping the peace. *(Looking out into the garden.)* Look at him out there now, showing off. He's still got that handkerchief tied round his eyes. Oh, my goodness, he's caught his finger on a thorn. *(Expletives come from the garden.)* You all right, dear? *(More expletives, louder.)* That's all right, then.

FIONA. Anyway, I don't suppose you'll divorce him because he's made a hole in the fence.

PAULINE. It's not his watching that worries me. It's Mr. Tovey. Middle-weight champion of the Royal Navy. And extremely jealous, they say. And Herbert ... well, he's never been one for keeping himself in trim.

FIONA. *(Rather relishing the prospect)* You mean there's a chance Mr. Tovey will come in here and beat father up?

PAULINE. I don't know about beat him up. But I hate scenes of any sort, even though I was on the stage.

Ringing of the front door bell.

FIONA. *(Immediately excited but calming herself)* That'll
    be Gerald. Now mother will you let him in? I want to
    stand here cool and aloof, and make a good impression.

PAULINE. All right. I hope it works. *(She goes out to
    front door.)*

*FIONA takes up dramatic and supposedly
attractive poses by the end of the settee,
never being quite satisfied, there is a
mumble of conversation in the hall and
then FIONA, with a gasp, flings herself
across the room and into the arms of the
... VICAR. PAULINE follows close behind him.*

FIONA. Oh, darling, I've been waiting so long for this
    moment ... *(realising her mistake)* Oh, Vicar!

VICAR. Well, I must say a vicar is not used to such a warm
    welcome these days.

FIONA. Oh, I'm sorry, Vicar.

PAULINE. Fiona, whatever made you do it?

VICAR. Oh, please Mrs. Farson, obviously for a moment
    I was mistaken for another. I am not complaining.

PAULINE. You two haven't met, have you?

VICAR. *(With a chortle)* I wouldn't say that.

PAULINE. But of course you know her. This is Fiona, our
    eldest daughter. Won't you sit down? You remember?

VICAR. *(Sitting on settee)* Oh, yes. I married the other
    three, didn't I, and christened their little ones.

PAULINE. We're all hoping that you'll be able to perform
    again for Fiona soon.

VICAR. Oh, how delightful. And are you hoping for a boy
    or a girl?

PAULINE. No, Vicar, you haven't got it right. Fiona's not
    married yet. But she's hoping to be.

VICAR. Dear me, dear me! But who am I to cast the first
    stone?

PAULINE. There's no need to cast any stones. Vicar.

VICAR. Quite, quite. But there are those among us who

delight in this vindictive occupation, are there not? It is the times, you know. I often think that great national paper is so aptly named ... The Times. There, too, in the announcements the births cometh before the marriages.

FIONA. *(Firmly)* I am not going to have a baby, Vicar.

VICAR. Oh, how sad. I am so sorry. And after looking forward to it for so long. But there will be other opportunities. You're still young ... *(He glances at her)* Well, fairly young. And your husband no doubt in the prime of life ...

FIONA. *(Annoyed with him)* I haven't got a husband yet.

VICAR. Who am I to cast the first stone, Mrs. Farson?

FIONA. Oh, God, this is where I came in. *(She slumps down on armchair U.L.)*

PAULINE. Oh, don't get so ruffled, dear. The Vicar can't be expected to know our little secrets, can he?

VICAR. I assure you not a word of this has reached me. Mrs. Throgmorton, my housekeeper, usually keeps me posted on local sin. I must speak to her about it.

PAULINE. I think you've got a bit confused, Vicar, between marriage and baptism.

VICAR. Have I really? *(Chortles)* That would never do, would it?

PAULINE. No. Now shall we start again.

VICAR. *(Confused).* Had we already started, then? I can't recall mentioning why I came. Are you sure?

PAULINE. Sure about what?

VICAR. Sure that I mentioned why I came.

PAULINE. No, I don't think you did.

VICAR. I thought you said we ought to start again.

PAULINE. Yes, I did.

VICAR. Please. Forgive me, I'm a little confused.

FIONA. *(Sarcastically)* I don't see why.

VICAR. If we are going to start again we must already have started, mustn't we. One must be logical. You agree?

PAULINE. *(Desperately)* Yes, Vicar, I agree to anything.

VICAR. Good. You see, they've got me to come and ask
    you'd be prepared to produce for us.

PAULINE. Produce what?

VICAR. Oh, just a little thing. I'm sure it won't put
    you   out at all. And you do have the experience.

PAULINE. Experience of what?

VICAR. Producing ... little things.

PAULINE. *(Who can hardly believe it)* I don't think that
    a very nice way to talk about my family, Vicar. I adm:
    to having had five daughters but I look on my children
    as gifts not as ... productions.

VICAR. Oh, dear me, please don't think I came here to
    ask you to produce another daughter ... I mean, at the
    drop of a hat.

PAULINE. You did say something about me having the
    experience.

VICAR. Experience of the theatre, dear Lady, not the ...
    Well, that's what I mean, anyway.

FIONA. I'm glad we've got that straight. I was getting
    worried.

PAULINE. I don't think my experience of the theatre ha
    got much to do with Fiona getting married.

VICAR. *(Confused again)* No, I don't suppose it has.
    (Pause) So you're getting married. Congratulations.
    I'm sure you'll make some man a very lucky wife, my
    dear.

FIONA. Gerald Dunjon. Do you know him? He has beer
    to a church he told me. It could have been yours, Vic:

VICAR. I'm not awfully good at remembering faces, I'm
    afraid.

FIONA. We're hoping to announce our engagement soor
    With any luck, this evening.

VICAR. Wonderful, wonderful! And when do you expec
    to be joined?

FIONA. Oh, quite soon after I should think.

VICAR. Let me have a date as soon as you can. The aut:
    will soon be upon us and in these days when so many

young people sow their wild oats I think it is advisable
that weddings should not coincide with the Harvest
Festival.

FIONA. *(Sharply)* Nothing like that, I assure you.

PAULINE. She'll want everything.

VICAR. I beg your pardon.

FIONA. I shall want the church bells.

VICAR. Oh, I'm sorry. I don't think you can have those.
They belong to the church, you see.

FIONA. I'd just love to hear them ringing, Vicar.

VICAR. Oh, you poor child! Deafness is a terrible afflic-
tion.

FIONA. Vicar, I can hear them if you ring them.

VICAR. But, my dear, no one can hear them if they are
not rung.

PAULINE. My daughter is simply making the point Vicar,
that she wants a ... a first-class wedding, with all the
trimmings.

FIONA. I shall want the choir, too, singing that hymn
that's been made into a pop number ... dare I mention
them, Vicar, the Beatles.

VICAR. Oh, they've done enormous damage in the church.
The rafters ...

FIONA. Not the beetles, Vicar. The Beatles.

VICAR. Just as you say.

FIONA. *(Rising)* Well, if you'll excuse me, I'll just have to
squeeze some lacquer out of your tin, mother. *(Moving
R.)* Hope to see you soon, Vicar. *(She goes out to hall
and upstairs.)*

VICAR. *(Looking after her)* Isn't her eyesight very good,
either?

PAULINE. There's nothing at all wrong with her, Vicar.

VICAR. Of course not. A charming girl ... er, woman. What
did you say her name was?

PAULINE. She's my daughter, Vicar.

VICAR. I'm not doubting it, Mrs. Farson. But I didn't
catch her name, I'm afraid.

PAULINE. Oh! Fiona.

VICAR. O'Fiona. That is unusual. Irish?

PAULINE. Scotch.

VICAR. Oh, that is kind of you. Just a little nip, then.

PAULINE gets up to oblige.

VICAR. Now, I've brought *The Little Woman* with me, outside in the car.

PAULINE. I didn't know you were married Vicar.

VICAR. I ought to have brought it in and showed you.

PAULINE. You'd never get a car in here.

VICAR. No, I know that. I was talking about the play.

PAULINE. What play's that, Vicar?

VICAR. You'd have a free hand.

PAULINE. Would I?

VICAR. Absolutely free.

PAULINE. Good.

VICAR. I'm so happy you accept, with your expertise we ought to win the Drama Festival this year. Thanks. *(He takes drink from her)* And I'm sure that you'll agree to my playing the juvenile lead ...

PAULINE. Have you done something in this line, then?

VICAR. Oh, yes, indeed. At school I was in *Othello,* They said I was the most remarkable Desdemona they ever seen. And up at the university I was in *Trouble A The Time.*

PAULINE. I suppose it was hushed up.

VICAR. Oh, Mrs. Farson, it wasn't as bad as all that. There was quite a good write-up in the Oxford Gazette.

PAULINE. I'd love to help you, Vicar. It would renew my youth to smell grease paint again. But I must speak to my husband first. *(Goes to french windows. Calls.)* Herbert! Herbert, darling, can you spare a moment or two?

HERBERT *(Off in garden)* What the blazes is it now?

PAULINE *(Very sweetly)* I want you, darling. *(Turning to VICAR)* He loves his garden.

VICAR. Ah, a garden is a loathsome thing, God wot.

PAULINE. What?

VICAR. Yes, wot. Curious old word, isn't it? *(Sees HERBERT at window.)* Oh!

HERBERT. *(Enters, still wearing his blindfold)* There! Does that satisfy you that I haven't been peeping?

PAULINE. Oh, Herbert, don't play games. The Vicar's here.

HERBERT. *(Tearing off handkerchief)* Oh, Hello, Vicar. Nice to see you. *(Explaining blindfold)* My eyes! Can't bear the sun, you know.

VICAR. But the sun's been gone an hour, Mr. Farson.

HERBERT. Has it really? Well, how was I to know with this thing on.

PAULINE. The Vicar wants me to direct a play for the Festival, dear. I thought I'd better ask you first.

HERBERT. Is there much in it?

VICAR. Just a one-act play, Mr. Farson. I daresay I shall play the lead..But perhaps Mrs. Farson could find you a small part.

HERBERT. I meant money-wise.

VICAR. Oh, good gracious, no. We all do it for love ... for love.

HERBERT. Well, I don't know. The stage sort of unbalances you, Pauline.

VICAR. I'm afraid you'd have to do without your dear wife on Monday and Thursday evenings ... rehearsal nights.

HERBERT. *(With a quick glance in the direction of the garden)* Oh, well ... I don't want to stand in her way.

VICAR. *(Rising)* Good. That's settled. Now if you'd like to pick up the book. *(Moves R.)* Nighty-nighty, Mr. Farson. *(To PAULINE as she accompanies him out into the hall.)* And if you could let me have the date of the christening as soon as possible ... *(VICAR AND PAULINE exit.. After a moment or two PAULINE returns carrying a copy of The Little Woman.)*

HERBERT. What's he talking about ... christening?
     You've been christened, haven't you?
PAULINE. Not me, Herbert, It's for Fiona.
HERBERT. *(Erupting)* What! Why haven't I been told?
     Why has it been kept so quiet?
PAULINE. *(With a smile)* Oh, no, dear. You've got the
     wrong end of the stick. It's the Vicar's fault, I'm
     afraid.
HERBERT. The Vicar! Oh, no, I'll never believe that.
PAULINE. He's such a busy man he gets confused
     occasionally. He actually meant to say wedding ...
     the wedding of Fiona and young Gerald Dunjon.
HERBERT. Oh! *(He hears the front door bell ringing.)*
     Talk of the little devil, that'll be him now.
PAULINE. Now be more tactful, Herbert. The last time he
     was here you kept on offering to lend him the money
     for the licence. Young men don't like to feel they're
     being bludgeoned into marriage. *(She goes out).*
HERBERT. *(Crosses to sideboard, muttering to himself)*
     If you didn't bludgeon them the world would be full
     of bachelors.
He is about to pour himself a drink but
GERALD is shown in by PAULINE.
PAULINE. It is Gerald, dear. And he arrived in a new car.
GERALD *(To HERBERT)* Good evening.. *(To PAULINE,*
     It's not a new car, Mrs. Farson. Just different.
PAULINE. That's what I meant, different.
HERBERT. *(Guffawing)* What's different about it? Does
     it run on water?
GERALD. Oh, very droll, Mr. Farson. Very droll. Quite
     witty.
HERBERT. You've got to be sharp-witted in my line. Now
     if you want tyres, lights, anything for the car, just give
     me a nod. Twenty-five per cent off for you, son.
PAULINE. I'll tell Fiona you're here. *(She goes out and
     upstairs).*
HERBERT. Well, sit down, Gerald. Make yourself at home

GERALD. Thanks. *(He sits on settee)*

HERBERT. New car, eh? You must be doing pretty well these days, Gerald. Be thinking of settling down soon, I expect.

GERALD. I'll have to settle up before I settle down.

HERBERT. *(After taking some time to see it)* Oh, very droll, Gerald, Very droll, Quite witty. *(Pause)* Now, Gerald, I must say that you and Fiona seem to be hitting it off and naturally ...

GERALD. Well, Mr. Farson, we haven't known each other very long and ...

HERBERT. Oh, long enough. You can always get to know a woman much better after you're married, you know. While you're just courting they keep such a lot hidden from you.

GERALD. I suppose you could say we're just good friends.

HERBERT. Oh, I don't want to stick my nose in where it's not wanted. It's simply that I couldn't go through again what I went through last March. She told you about Johnny Spinet?

GERALD. She did say she'd once known someone of that name who'd left town.

HERBERT. Just as well for him he did.

GERALD. I'm not going to worry myself about what Fiona was doing six months ago, Mr. Farson.

HERBERT. She didn't do anything, poor girl. It was what was done to her ... or strictly speaking, not done to her, ... that caused me so much grief and anguish. Never again, I swore. Never again. Do you know we were actually standing at the church door long enough for her bouquet to wilt in her hand? I was there to give her away. But there was no one to give her to. Can you think of anything more heartless, Gerald?

GERALD. I'll try ... but ... no, off-hand I don't think I can.

HERBERT. If she was let down a second time do you

know what I'd do?

GERALD. Get her to try again, I suppose: third time lucky.

HERBERT. *(Exploding)* No, I would not. I'd get hold of the man who'd let her down ... oh, yes I would, even if it meant following him to the ends of the earth ... and then I'd rip him to pieces with my bare hands. *(He demonstrates. GERALD reacts.)* Well, you understand father's feelings.

GERALD. I'm afraid not.

HERBERT. *(Shouting angrily)* And why not?

GERALD. Well, I'm not a father.

HERBERT. You know what I'm talking about. You're not daft.

GERALD. If you think I've said anything about marriage to Fiona ...

HERBERT. You don't have to say anything, son. Actions speak louder than words. Now, I know ... and you know ... that when a young chap starts paying out on a girl that's not friendship any longer. That's an investment. He's waiting for the interest to be paid. Am I right?

GERALD. If you say so.

HERBERT. There's nothing personal in all this.

GERALD. Oh, good!

HERBERT. Nothing personal at all. It wouldn't make any difference to me if it was you or someone else. I'd have his guts for garters no matter who it was.

PAULINE. *(Entering from hall)* She's just coming, Gerald. And she looks radiant this evening. Just like a bride.

HERBERT. That's how we wanted her to look. Isn't it, Gerald?

PAULINE. Going somewhere nice?

GERALD. A spin in the new car ... no, not new ... different car out to Gresham Mill.

PAULINE. You can always come back here.

GERALD. *(A trifle suspiciously)* Can we?

PAULINE. Herbert and I are going over to Aunt Melinda's

We won't be back until eleven. That's right, Herbert,
isn't it? Eleven.

HERBERT. Yes, that's right. *(Making it very clear.)* We
won't get back here a minute before eleven.

GERALD. Oh, well, have a good time.

PAULINE. Same to you, I'm sure.

HERBERT. But not too good a time.

FIONA. *(Coming downstairs and entering from hall)* Oh,
darling, I hope I haven't kept you waiting.

GERALD. No. Your father has been ... entertaining me.

HERBERT. That's right *(He gives PAULINE a nudge)*
Now Gerald, I'd like you to go and have a look at my
Isaac Perrier.

GERALD. Your what, Mr. Farson?

PAULINE. *(Who has now got the idea, taking GERALD's
arm)* Don't look so alarmed, Gerald It's only a rose.
*(And singing Only A Rose she takes GERALD off to
garden.)*

FIONA. Well, Dad, that was pretty obvious, I must say.

HERBERT. Can't he helped. I want a word with you
before you go out.

FIONA. *(Rather wearily seating herself on settee)* Oh,
no, Dad. Not the same old warning.

HERBERT. Yes. But more so. Listen, I've softened him
up. He's feeling a little punch drunk right at this
moment. This evening, girl, you've got to move in for
the kill.

FIONA. Oh, Dad, you make it sound so clinical.

HERBERT. I'm telling you he's a pushover. If you want
him you've only got to move in now and take him.

FIONA. I don't know if I can. He's got a mind of his own,
you know.

HERBERT. Good gracious girl, once you turn on your ...
appeal ... well, even Einstein's mind wouldn't count
for much

FIONA. What do you mean by appeal?

HERBERT. Fiona, you're ... well, you're somewhere

between twenty-eight and thirty-five, according to
which way you calculate it ... you don't want to waste
time on sparring. You want this fellow to marry you.
Now I would have thought it was common knowledge.

FIONA. I know how to make myself pleasant, I hope.

HERBERT. Who wants a pleasant girl? You've got to be
irresistible . To be irresistible you might have to get
downright unpleasant.

FIONA. It was so different with Johnny, The second time
we were together he came straight out with it: "Will
you marry me?" Just like that.

HERBERT. He was a damned sight better at proposing
than actually marrying. This fellow's the other way
round. He'll be keen enough in the end, you'll see.
Look, imagine him as a man dying of thirst in the
desert. You appear. You hold up the life-saving water
before his eyes. But you don't give it to him see?

FIONA. No?

HERBERT. No. You say, 'If you want it you walk across
here, old son, and get it.' I've put it into an allergy
but I'm sure you know what I'm getting at.

FIONA. The thing is, can I make him thirsty enough?

HERBERT. I don't doubt it. Nature, in her infinite
wisdom, has dealt women all the trumps. Now come
on, smile! I'm sure that when your mother and I come
home tonight you're going to announce your
engagement.

FIONA. I do hope your right.

HERBERT. *(Crossing to window)*There's going to be a
bloody row if you don't. *(Calling into garden.)* Fiona's
waiting, young man. Oh, look what your mother's
doing, boarding up that gap in the fence. Leave that
fence alone!

GERALD. *(Entering from garden)* Lovely, Mr. Farson.

HERBERT. Did you have a look through?

GERALD. I was talking about your roses. You must put
in a lot of time in your garden.

HERBERT. Quite a bit, here and there. *(Winks at FIONA)* But the secret is water, plenty of water.

FIONA. That reminds me, Dad, that cistern is leaking again.

HERBERT. I know. Your mother's sent for the man.

FIONA. That chewing gum you used to mend it must have come out.

HERBERT. Get along now. I'm sure Gerald doesn't want a lecture on hydraulics.

GERALD. No, thanks. *(To FIONA)* I thought we might run out to Gresham Mill and back. *(PAULINE enters from garden.)*

FIONA. Plenty of water there.

HERBERT. You make sure there is.

GERALD. Well, goodbye Mrs. Farson, Mr. Farson.

FIONA. Bye, bye. *(FIONA and GERALD go out into hall. A moment later the front door is shut and then a car starts up.)*

PAULINE. You're a ruthless man, Herbert.

HERBERT. *(Taking it as a compliment)* I don't deny it. That's how I've got on in the world.

PAULINE *(Scornfully)* What! Living on Unemployment Pay and National assistance for the past four years.

HERBERT. *(Quite unabashed)* And don't forget that with all my little fiddles I've never paid a penny in Income Tax. It's not easy, you know.

PAULINE. I'm not so sure you don't put a young man off marriage.

HERBERT. Listen, mother. What I do I do for the sake of my children. Face the fact ... Fiona is incapable of getting a man to the altar off her own bat. She's been half-way up the aisle on a dozen occasions and never once made the starting-gate. And time's not on her side. She's on the verge of Old Maidenhood. This may be her last chance.

PAULINE. I don't think we ought to interfere.

HERBERT. We're not interfering. We're simply making

sure she pulls it off this time. *(Pause)* Now I'm going up to tidy round the back bedroom. *(Innocently whistling he walks towards the hall.)*

PAULINE. *(Handing him binoculars from sideboard)* Here. *(With a long-suffering sigh.)* I daresay you'll want these.

As HERBERT shame-facedly takes the binoculars.

The Curtain Falls

ACT ONE

Scene Two.*The same, about ten o'clock that evening.*
When the curtain rises the stage is empty and in darkness.
The front door is opened and the hall light switched on.
There is a murmur of conversation in the hall and then
JENNY appears and switches on the room lights.

JENNY. Come on in, Derek. There's no one about.

DEREK. *(Hobbling in)* Silly blessed thing to do. I didn't
see the step.

JENNY. Does it hurt a lot?

DEREK. It's a bit sore.

JENNY. I'd better take a look at it.

DEREK. It's just below my knees.

JENNY. I don't care where it is. It'll have to be cleaned.

DEREK. *(Sitting on settee and rolling up his trouser leg)*
There! Nothing really. Nothing to make a fuss about.

JENNY. *(Insisting on being helpful)* That doesn't look
too good to me.

DEREK. It's not there. It's lower down.

JENNY. Oh, that is a nasty graze

DEREK. *(Humouring her)* Go on with you. I've had
worse wounds than that through shaving.

JENNY. *(Innocently)* Do you shave your legs, then?

DEREK. Darling, you musn't fuss over me.

JENNY. Supposing the dye came out of those trousers
and got in there. See, you didn't think of that, did
you?

DEREK. I must admit it hadn't worried me unduly.

JENNY. You've got to take better care of yourself. Or

have someone do it for you.

DEREK. You're a kind soul, Jenny, but really I can patch that up when I get back to the yacht.

JENNY. And all that time have the bacteria working away at you ... destroying the tissues.

DEREK. I shouldn't think they'd bother.

JENNY. You can't be too careful. This is a very bad area for bacteria, My sister Teresa fell off a swing in the garden once. And she couldn't sit down for a month. All because something got in there.

DEREK. *(Tapping his knee)* You really think something's got in there, do you? In the dark?

JENNY. I'm going to clean it whether you like it or not. *(She moves towards exit).* Like all the boys you're a bit of a coward, aren't you? Now you just sit still. *(She goes out and turns to her right in hall towards the kitchen.)*

After a few moments DEREK looks anxiously at his watch.

DEREK. *(Calling to her)* I haven't got a lot of time, darling.

JENNY. *(Off)* I'm just coming.

DEREK stands and flexes his leg. It is a bit stiff and he winces.

JENNY. *(Entering with small bowl of water, towel and First Aid kit in a large tin marked with a red cross)* I told you to sit still.

DEREK. *(Shamefacedly)* Sorry. *(He sits.)*

JENNY. *(Placing tin, bowl and towel before settee)* Now you've got nothing to worry about. I was in the Girl Guides. *(She opens the tin and removes dressing, plaster, bandages and scissors and lays them out on the floor.)*

DEREK. What are you going to do, amputate?

JENNY. I'm going to make sure this is clean and properly dressed.

She is about to start when she notices that —

*the curtains to the french windows are
open. She goes over to them and pulls
them across.*

DEREK. It's a secret operation, eh?

JENNY. *(Returning to D.C. and kneeling by her first aid
kit)* I don't want the whole world looking in at me
playing with your knee.

DEREK. *(In mock alarm)* Playing with it?

JENNY. *(As she cleans the wound and applies a dressing
and bandage)* Oh, you know what I mean.

DEREK. You've got such wonderfully gentle hands.

JENNY. *(Delighted by this compliment)* Have I really?

DEREK. *(Wincing as she hurts him)* Yes, you'd have made
a first-class blacksmith.

JENNY. *(Annoyed)* Derek, you're always taking the
micky.

DEREK. Not really. I am grateful. And you're a lovely
girl, you know.

JENNY. Yes I know, I've heard that said many times.

DEREK. Oh, have you really? By whom?

JENNY. I talk to myself quite a bit.

They Laugh

DEREK. *(More serious)* I'm really very sorry about the
way things turned out this evening.

JENNY. I enjoyed it. It was enough for me just being
with you.

DEREK. It wasn't what I planned. Just bad luck to run
into that bore Elvira.

JENNY. She's very svelte.

DEREK. That's her trouble. She's svelte too much.

JENNY. She said you were considering her for a part in
your film.

DEREK. She was trying to make you jealous, my pet.
If I ever do one on *Bloodsuckers of the
South Coast*   she'll probably get the lead. But in
this film ... nothing. I've told you that you're the
ideal girl for the part.

JENNY. I do hope I can please you.

DEREK. You'll please me all right.

JENNY. You've got what they call latent ability. And I'm just the man to bring it out.

JENNY. Oh, I hope so. There, how's that?

DEREK. Fine. *(Testing his leg by standing)* Wouldn't know I had a leg at all.

JENNY. It's just a precaution. *(Rises and moves with bowl and towel towards exit.)*

DEREK. Very wise to take precautions.

JENNY. Help yourself to a drink. *(She goes out to kitchen.)*

DEREK, intending to do so takes a few steps in the direction of the sideboard and falls over the first-aid tin.

JENNY. *(Rushing back into the room)* What happened? Did it give out?

DEREK. Yes. It was a mistake not to issue me with crutches.

JENNY. *(As she helps him up)* Oh, it was my fault, You fell over the First-Aid tin.

DEREK. *(With a brave smile)* Could there be a more appropriate place?

JENNY. *(Anxious)* You're not hurt?

DEREK. Only because you must think me a clumsy idiot.

JENNY. *(Infatuated)* I think you're wonderful.

DEREK. *(After staring into her large, adoring eyes for a few moments. She seems to be expecting a kiss. He breaks away)* Yes, well, I think I'll have that drink now. How about you?

JENNY. *(Breaking down L. Disappointed)* I never do.

DEREK. Never?

JENNY. If this meeting with the Duke goes well tonight and you make this film on wild life conservation I'll have a little sip with you tomorrow to celebrate.

DEREK. *(As he pours himself a Scotch at Sideboard R.)* That'll have to be after the test.

JENNY. *(Excited, as she packs up First-Aid kit in tin and pushes tin under table in C. back)* You're going to test me tomorrow?

DEREK. I want the backers to see you on film as soon as possible. Once I get their okay, you're in.

JENNY. Do I have to go to London?

DEREK. That won't be necessary. The stateroom on my yacht can be fixed up as a studio. I'll do the test there Come down in the afternoon.

JENNY. About two?

DEREK. Fine. I'll fix up a bed and you can do your stuff.

JENNY. There won't be anyone else there?

DEREK. Why?

JENNY. I'd be embarrassed.

DEREK. No, there'll only be me. I'm quite capable of operating the equipment. If you like I could take the boat out a couple of miles, then no one would hear you scream.

JENNY. *(As though she regards the idea as childish)* Derek, I won't scream.

DEREK. I'm afraid you've got to. The scene calls for it.

JENNY. Oh, I see. And what do I have to wear?

DEREK. You'll be in bed, so not much.

JENNY. And this girl's in bed and her lover ... that's Modigliani ... is leaving her.

DEREK. That's right. We don't see Modigliani in this shot. Just you, sitting up in bed, realising you're about to be abandoned, and stretching out your arms in a last supplication.

JENNY. It's going to be great fun.

DEREK. That's settled then.

JENNY. I can't tell you how much I'm looking forward to tomorrow afternoon.

DEREK. Me, too.

JENNY. It might be a turning point in my life.

DEREK. More than likely. Well, thanks for the drink. But

I must make a move now.

JENNY. *(Suddenly, with a cry)* Oh, Look! you've got a hole in your leg.

DEREK. *(Alarmed)* A hole? What, right through?

JENNY. In your trouser leg.

DEREK. Oh, God!

JENNY. I bet that was caused by the First-Aid tin.

DEREK. Yes, dangerous things, aren't they? *(Looking at his watch)* I haven't got time to get another pair from the yacht.

JENNY. You can't go and meet the Duke like that. *(Slight pause for thought)* Sit down again.

DEREK. *(Obeying her, sitting on settee)* What are you going to do?

JENNY. *(Getting needle and cotton from sideboard drawer)* Mend them, of course.

DEREK. I suppose it would be disrespectful appearing before the Duke in rented trousers ... trousers with a rent in them, I mean.

JENNY. *(Crossing to settee and pulling his leg onto her lap)* Scandalous. Now, keep your leg still. *(She begins to sew)*.

DEREK. *(After watching her nimble fingers for a while)* I don't like the way that needle goes flashing in and out.

JENNY. As long as it comes out each time you've nothing to worry about. Oh, what's wrong here? *(She tugs at the trouser leg.)* Oh, damn, I've sewn it to the bandage.

DEREK. That's fine, Jenny. Really.

JENNY. You can't go like that. It's all puckered up. *(She rips the trouser leg away from the bandage.)* Look, I can't do it with them on.

DEREK. Eh.

JENNY. Go behind that chair and slip them off. I won't look. Then I'll take them up to my room and fix them on my machine.

DEREK. I don't know if I ought to.

JENNY. Oh, go on. Don't be so embarrassed.

DEREK. *(Doing as he is told, handing her the trousers from his cover behind the armchair U.L.)* Here you are. Don't be too long, darling, will you? *(As she moves away)* I hope your mother and father don't turn up.

JENNY. Relax. They won't be back for another hour yet. *(SHE goes out and upstairs.)*

After a little while DEREK ventures from behind the chair, Crosses to sideboard and pours himself a drink which he swallows quickly. Sees the transistor radio standing on the sideboard and switches it on. It plays part of Swan Lake Ballet music. DEREK beats times with his foot and finally breaks into a few steps of Ballet. He rather fancies himself and lets himself go. His dance is interrupted by the banging of the front door. He flees and takes cover behind the armchair U.K. His head appears above his folded arms on the back of the chair.

PAULINE enters. She switches off the radio.

PAULINE. Oh, that Jenny. *(Blaming her for leaving the radio on. She looks at herself in the mirror and gives her hair a pat. She sees DEREK's reflection and turns, surprised)* Oh, ... er ... hullo!

DEREK. How do you do?

PAULINE. *(Not knowing what to say)* Still uncomfortably hot, isn't it?

DEREK. Decidedly cooler, I thought.

PAULINE. *(Having decided that the visitor must have come to see HERBERT)* My husband won't be long. He's just putting the car away.

DEREK. *(Hurriedly)* Oh, please tell him not to hurry on my account.

PAULINE. *(After a pause)* Won't you sit down?

DEREK. No, no. I prefer to stand. *(Pause)* I actually like

standing.

As PAULINE moves D.S. DEREK manouevres the
chair so that his undressed legs remain hidden
from her.

PAULINE. *(After a pause, a bit doubtfully)* Is it about the
    cistern?

DEREK. Oh, ... er ... is it?

PAULINE. We expected you this afternoon.

DEREK. Oh, did you?

PAULINE. It is an emergency. I made that clear. Perhaps
    you'd better come up and have a look at it. *(She moves*
    towards hall doorway.)

DEREK. I'd ... I'd rather not ... at the moment.

PAULINE. Now look at those curtains pulled. And it's
    stifling in here. *(She is about to cross him to french*
    windows.)

DEREK. *(In panic)* No, please don't touch them. (She
    looks at him in astonishment.) Please. I ... I ... think
    I've got pheumonia coming on.

PAULINE. Pneumonia! Do you think you should be out,
    then?

DEREK. I ... I ... wish I wasn't, really.

HERBERT enters from hall.

HERBERT. I can hear Jenny up in her room busy on her
    machine. Another new dress, I suppose. *(Sees DEREK)*
    Oh!

PAULINE. This is the man from the plumber's dear. About
    the cistern.

HERBERT. We asked for you about eight hours ago. We
    might be under six foot of water by now.

DEREK. That would be nice.

PAULINE. Not with pneumonia, it wouldn't.

HERBERT. What are you talking about? *(Crosses quickly*
    to french windows.) Look at those curtains. And it's
    Stifling in here. *(He pulls curtains, turns and sees DEREK*
    who, cannot hide himself from PAULINE and HERBERT
    At the same time, draws curtains to.) Stand back, mother

This man's got no trousers on.

PAULINE. Are you sure? *(She moves forward)*

HERBERT. Stand back, I said.

PAULINE. You're not from the plumber's. You don't know anything about cisterns, do you.

DEREK. I wish I could say I did.

PAULINE. What are you doing in my house dressed like that .... I mean, undressed like that?

HERBERT. Leave this to me, mother.

DEREK. I know it looks queer but my trousers are upstairs. Your daughter ... well, I presume you are her father ...

HERBERT. *(Furious at the imagined insult)* What are you implying mister?

DEREK. *(Hurriedly)* I'm not implying anything. I'm only trying to explain. You see, I fell over the First Aid kit.

PAULINE. Ours? The one that's kept on the top shelf of the cupboard. *(She points in the direction of the kitchen.)*

DEREK. Believe me, this has never happened to me before. I mean being found like this ... by ... by ... by parents.

HERBERT *(Taking off his jacket)* There's a first time for everything. And a last.

DEREK. But it wouldn't have happened if you'd come back a bit later.

HERBERT. God knows what would have happened if we'd come back a bit later.

DEREK. Call Jenny down and get her to explain.

HERBERT. Go on, Pauline, get her down. *(PAULINE goes into the hall and calls for JENNY.)* I'll deal with my daughter, later. *(He begins to roll up his shirt-sleeves)* But now I intend to thrash you within an inch of your life, sir.

DEREK. What, now?

HERBERT. Can you think of a better time?

DEREK. *(Cringeing)* Yes, Yes, I think I can.

As HERBERT advances upon DEREK, JENNY,
carrying the repaired trousers enters, followed
by PAULINE.

JENNY. *(Dashing in)* Oh, daddy, don't hit him. You don
understand. I made him take his trousers off.

PAULINE. Oh, my God! My own daughter! Come per-
missive like all the rest of them.

JENNY. Don't dramatise, mother. Here Derek, slip these
on. *(Handing the trousers to DEREK. To PAULINE
and HERBERT.)* I had to mend them before he left
this house, that 's all.

PAULINE. *(Whimpering)* I don't know if I want to know

JENNY. What you've seen is not what it looks like.
Perhaps I'd better introduce you. This is Derek Colbert
the film producer. Derek, my mother and father.

DEREK. Please to meet you. *(Struggling to get his
trousers on behind the chair he has got the left leg in
the right leg of the trousers and as he straightens up
he trips and falls over.)*

JENNY. *(Hurrying to his aid)* Derek, are you all right?

HERBERT. *(Preventing her)* Don't touch him. *(Watching
DEREK's desperate struggles)* Look, he doesn't even
know how to put trousers on. Words fail me.

JENNY. Good!

HERBERT. Now listen, you. I'll give you ten seconds to
get out of this house. Ten seconds dead. *(He begins
to count like a boxing referee.)*

JENNY. Oh, don't make such a fuss, daddy. I was mending his trousers because he'd fallen down.

HERBERT. What do you mean, they'd fallen down?
Trousers don't fall down that easily.

DEREK. No. I'd fallen down. I'm a bit accident prone,
I'm afraid.

HERBERT. *(Advancing with menace)* You can say that
again.

DEREK. No. Wait. You see, I've got this important meeting with The Duke to discuss how we can keep wild animals from being wiped out and ... I'm hoping to make a film about it.

HERBERT. I don't know how you've got the gall to think up these excuses.

JENNY. It's not an excuse, daddy.

HERBERT. Then it damned well ought to be! Now you, Out!

JENNY. I'll see you to the door.

HERBERT. *(Pulling her back.)* Oh, no, you don't! I'm directing this scene. *(He pushes DEREK towards the hall door.)*

DEREK. *(As he passes JENNY)* Arrangements stand, Jenny.

JENNY. Okay, Derek.

HERBERT. Come on, you! Out!

HERBERT propels DEREK out into the hall a moment or two later the front door is heard to slam.

PAULINE. Oh, Jenny, I never thought I'd live to see the day when ...

JENNY. Of all the ridiculous fuss! Why is it that the older generation is so guilt-laden that it sees the worst in everything?

PAULINE. Oh, don't call me the 'older generation', dear. I've always tried to be trendy for my children's sake.

JENNY. Well, I'm off, to bed.

HERBERT. *(Entering in a fury)* Where are you going?

JENNY. To bed. Goodnight.

JERBERT. No, wait. I've got a few bones to pick with you my girl.

PAULINE. Pick them in the morning, dear. At breakfast time.

HERBERT. After this I won't be able to eat any breakfast, Pauline.

PAULINE. *(All out to placate him)* Yes, you will dear.
   Because you're a kind and just man and you'll come to
   realise that Jenny can stand up to all the world and
   say, This was a man. *(She has obviously lost herself.
   Sheepishly)* That's the end of Julius Ceasar.
HERBERT. *(After recovering from his wife's excursion
   into inconsequence)* And this is the end of this Derek
   Cobblers ... or whatever his name is. I forbid you to see
   him again, Jenny. *(JENNY is silent)* Now don't argue.
PAULINE. Your father has spoken, dear.
HERBERT. And I mean what I say. Never again. On pain
   of ... well, I wouldn't strike you..But as for him, I
   promise you you won't recognise him ... with or without
   trousers.
JENNY. *(Calmly and shortly)* Goodnight, then. *(She goes
   out and upstairs.)*
HERBERT. *(Comes C. sinks onto settee)* Oh, my God! Why
   did I have five daughters!
PAULINE..I had them, actually, dear.
HERBERT. Oh, I'm not blaming you. But it's such a delicate
   matter bringing up daughters. Up to a certain age you've
   got to protect them from men and then, a few years later
   you're looking around for any poor stoodge who's daft
   enough to take them off your hands. *(Suddenly lively
   again.)* That reminds me. What's the time?
PAULINE. You'll get one if you hurry.
HERBERT. Get one? What are you talking about?
PAULINE. A pint at the *WHITE BEAR*. Isn't that ...?
HERBERT. You're always thinking about physical pleasure
   Pauline. I'm thinking about that couple that were running
   out to Gresham Mill. They ought to be home any minute
   now.
PAULINE. Oh, yes, I wonder how she's getting on.
HERBERT. I think we'd better go on up. We can listen from
   the landing. Then at the right moment... The physiologic
   moment ... we can come down here and confront them.
   He won't be able to deny it, you see, and then we'll have

him where .... *(Front door is closed)* My God, that's the
door. They're here.

PAULINE. They musn't find us ... we shall spoil everything
for her ... Oh, my ....

HERBERT. *(A picture of panic)* Don't lose your head woman
Behind the curtains ... Quick. *(They hide behind the curtains of the french windows. Once there, HERBERT pokes
his head and arm out to grab his jacket. At that moment
FIONA enters and sees him).*

FIONA. Come on in, Gerry darling. Oh, the light's on.
That's that little brat Jenny, I bet.

GERALD. *(As he enters)* You're quite sure your people
aren't home yet?

FIONA. They said eleven, darling. We've got three-quarters
of an hour. I know you. You can do quite a lot in three-
quarters of an hour.

GERALD. I'm not denying it, But can't you make sure? I'd
feel a bit more relaxed if I knew we weren't likely to be
disturbed by Sarah Bernhardt and Il Duce.

FIONA. Oh, don't speak about mummy and daddy like that,
darling. It's not fair when they dote on you so much.

GERALD. Sorry. *(He crosses and stands with his back to
the curtains.)* Still, there are times when I don't want then
breathing down my neck.

FIONA. Okay, I'll nip upstairs and check. You make yoursel
comfortable.

*FIONA goes out and upstairs. Directly he is alone
GERALD takes his jacket off and hangs it on the
back of the chair U.L. He rubs his hands together
in gleeful anticipation. It is a bit hot. He takes his
tie off. FIONA re-enters.*

FIONA. No, they're not home yet. And Jenny's asleep. At
least she's locked herself in her room.

GERALD. Good show. Decks all cleared for action, eh?

DIONA. Oh, Gerry darling, you are keen.

GERALD. And why not? I'm young and you're ... er ...
beautiful.

FIONA. You didn't waste much time in divesting.

GERALD. It's so hot in here. Couldn't we draw the curtains and open up the windows. *(He moves to do this)*

FIONA. *(Hurriedly stopping him)* No, don't do that.

GERALD. Why not? Think how this heat is sapping my energy.

FIONA. *(Stopping him as he makes another attempt to pull the curtains.)* No, that terrible Mr. Tovey next door is always trying to see in here.

GERALD. Then we could put the lights out.

FIONA. I'm afraid in the dark.

GERALD. You wouldn't be afraid of me, would you?

FIONA. In the mood you're in, any girl would be a bit scared.

GERALD. *(Flattered)* Do I really have that effect on you baby? *(He takes her hand and leads her to the settee.)*

FIONA. You know you do. Every time you touch me I go weak at the knees. *(They sit on the settee)*

GERALD. You're going to be very floppy, then, by the time I've finished with you. *(They kiss)* How's that? Old patella beginning to go?

FIONA. It is the same for you, isn't it?

GERALD. What is?

FIONA. Do your knees go like jelly when I've got my arms around you?

GERALD. Haven't you noticed? I can hardly keep from lying down.

FIONA. I do think there is something between us, don't you?

GERALD. *(Moving with discomfort, and rubbing his leg)* Yes, it's this bit of wood down the middle of the settee. Where did you get this thing? Out of a model village?

FIONA. It is a bit small. But then you use such a lot of it.

GERALD. Might have had more room if we'd stayed in

the car.

FIONA. What did you mean when you kept saying my slip was clutching?

GERALD. *(With a short laugh)* I didn't say that. I said her clutch was slipping.

FIONA. Oh, I'm sorry. I don't really know anything about clutches.

GERALD. *(Embracing her)* I wouldn't say that.

FIONA. *(Pushing him off)* Gerry, darling, I want to ask you a serious question.

GERALD. Has it got to be now?

FIONA. Yes, it has. Well, are you serious?

GERALD. Is that the question?

FIONA. Sometimes you don't seem very serious. And I want to know if you're serious ... about me.

GERALD. Do you know you're different tonight. I can almost hear your brain ticking.

FIONA. It's only that I want to be one hundred per cent sure of you.

GERALD..Oh, you don't have to worry about that.

FIONA. I'll be frank. I think we've gone about as far as we can go on ... how shall I put it? on a hit or miss basis.

GERALD. Have you been reading Marjorie Proops?

FIONA. Please, darling, be serious. If you wanted me as you say you do you'd be prepared to commit yourself.

GERALD. I love you, Fiona. Love you. Love you. Love you How's that?

FIONA. How much do you love me?

GERALD..More than I can say.

FIONA. No, go on. Say it. Try.

GERALD. I don't know if I can, sweetheart. I'm not very demonstrative. *(But his acrobatics on the settee as he embraces FIONA gives the lie to this statement. Suddenly in the middle of the kiss, he lets out a piercing shriek.)* Oh, God, it's happened again.

FIONA. *Alarmed as GERALD throws himself in agony about the settee)* What have I done *(GERALD is*

grasping his thigh and wincing in pain.) I didn't touch
anything.

GERALD. No, it's not you.

FIONA. Oh, Gerry, don't make those horrible faces.

GERALD. *(Gasping)* My leg! Ouch! Coo, it's bad. *(He
wimpers in pain)*

FIONA. What's happened?

GERALD. Cramp. I've got cramp. It's this bloody little
settee.

FIONA. Cramp! Push your leg out straight.

GERALD. *(Testily because he has got his leg out straight)*
If I get it any straighter it'll be a foot longer than the
other one.

FIONA. Stand up. *(GERALD does so.)* Put your weight
on your heel. Walk about a bit. *(FIONA watches with
concern as GERALD executes a strange walk.)* Is it
going off?

GERALD. *(At last)* I think so. My gosh, that was bad. I
suffer a bit from cramp. Circulation's all up the wall.
Ought to get it re-routed.

FIONA. *(Taking his arm)* You'll be all right. I'll look
after you.

GERALD. I'm sorry about that Fiona. You must think
I'm a pretty rotten lover, stiffening up like a board
when I'm supposed to be floppy as jelly.

FIONA. *(Leading him back to settee)* We can't always
plan these things, darling. You couldn't help it. Now ta
it easy.   *(They sit on the settee, GERALD turned
away from the curtains.)*

GERALD. Must have been the power of your kiss honey.
Went straight down my leg and tightened up all my
muscles.

FIONA. In that case, I'd better not kiss you again.

GERALD. It wasn't quite fatal. I think I can risk another
(He kisses her)

FIONA. *(After a pause)* You know what the trouble is
darling?

GERALD. Yes, it's this rotten settee. Never made for amorous acrobatics.

FIONA. No, we're too tense here. If only we had a place of our own.

GERALD. I've told you. You can always come round to the flat. I'll get Peter to make himself scarce for the evening.

FIONA. I don't like that sort of talk, Gerald. It cheapens me.

GERALD. Sorry. Just trying to be helpful.

FIONA. I meant a place that belonged to you and me.

GERALD. Take a flat together. That's a great idea.

FIONA. I meant ... get married.

GERALD. *(Pulled up with a jerk)* Oh!

FIONA. Well, what do you say?

GERALD. Fiona, do you think it's possible for a man to love a girl so much that marriage would be an anticlimax?

FIONA. *(Emphatically)* No!

GERALD. I didn't think you would.

FIONA. I want to get married. It's so obviously the solution. And you want it, too, if you'd only face up to it.

GERALD. I've nothing against marriage.

FIONA. Oh, good, when?

GERALD. I thought, perhaps in three or four years' time. When I'm more mature.

FIONA. *(Disgusted with him)* You're mature enough now. I ought to know.

GERALD. Why all this interest in marriage this evening? Your father was on about it earlier. I didn't take a lot of notice. With all due respect, darling, he is a bit of an old windbag, isn't he?

HERBERT's face contorted with rage appears from between the curtains. PAULINE pulls him back. There is a momentary scuffle behind the curtains. FIONA, but not GERALD has seen this.

FIONA Oh, Gerald, I can't wait three or four years. It's not fair to ask me, wanting you the way I do.

GERALD And I want you, darling. Let's not think about marriage. Let's not think about ourselves.

FIONA I would like that. Really I would.

GERALD. Come on, then.

FIONA. *(Pushing him away)* No wait a minute.

GERALD. *(Attempting to embrace her)* Darling, you talk too much. You're wasting time. Your folks'll be back soon.

FIONA. *(Struggling free)* Just one second.

GERALD. What is it now?

FIONA. *(Getting to her feet)* I'll slip and bolt on the front door and on the back door so we can't be surprised.

GERALD. Ah, now you're getting the idea, honey. Hurry up, then.

FIONA goes into the hall. We hear the bolt pushed home on the front door. She appears at the doorway on her way to the back door.

FIONA. *(Looking in)* Won't be a second. *(She goes out to back door and bolts it).*

GERALD has not wasted his time. He has been arranging cushions on the small settee and testing his length on it. It is unsatisfactory; he arranged the cushions on the floor in front of the settee. He is lying on the floor when FIONA returns.

GERALD. *(Stretching up his arms to her)* Darling!

FIONA. *(Keeping clear of him on the far side of the settee)* I'm worried.

GERALD. Nothing to be worried about. Come on. Come to Daddy.

FIONA. No, Daddy. You wait.

GERALD. *(Getting impatient)* What's the matter now?

FIONA. You don't seem any different from all the other

men I've known. You've only one thing on your mind, haven't you?

GERALD. *(Protesting)* But no, darling.

FIONA. Name something else, then?

GERALD. What?

FIONA. Something else on your mind.

GERALD. What? Like that? Off the cuff?

FIONA. You can't can you.?

GERALD. But naturally my mind's full of thoughts of you darling. And how I can make you happy.

FIONA. You can make me happy by showing me that you're not like other men.

GERALD. But, of course, I'm not like other men. *(Pause for thought)* Well, I'm like them in some ways ... but I'd never think of taking advantage.

FIONA. I'm so glad you're genuine.

GERALD. Come on, then, darling. No more doubts.

FIONA. If we could regard ourselves as sort of engaged I wouldn't think it so awfully wrong.

GERALD. *(Eagerly)* Well, in that case, consider yourself engaged.

FIONA. *(Coming round the front of settee. Sits)* I think you'd better make it sound a bit more romantic, darling. Just to put my mind at ease.

GERALD. All right. I love you and we can consider ourselves engaged. Now come on, darling. Let's not waste any more time. *(He tries to pull her down onto the floor but she successfully resists him.)*

FIONA. That's not quite right, is it? I think you ought to propose to me properly. A girl does expect these little courtesies. Even when you know what the answer's going to be.

GERALD. Okay, if that's what you want. *(He kneels before her)* Darling, Fiona, will you marry me?

FIONA. *(Quickly)* Yes, Gerry, I will.

GERALD. Good. Now the formalities are over let's celebrate.

GERALD is about to pull FIONA down to him on the
floor when HERBERT and PAULINE burst into
the room from behind the curtains.

HERBERT. *(Coming R.C. as if to cut off GERALD's*
    retreat from the room should that be contemplated)
    I heard that. I heard that. Congratulations, my boy.

PAULINE. *As she follows HERBERT in)* Oh, Gerald,
    how happy you've made us.

FIONA. *(Pretending surprise)* Mum, Dad, wherever did
    you spring from?

PAULINE. The doors were bolted. We came in through
    the french windows.

GERALD. *(Helplessly)* I thought the windows were shut.

HERBERT. I've got a knack of opening them. Anyway,
    what's it matter? We were just in time, weren't we?

PAULINE. It was a lovely proposal, Gerald. You must
    have rehearsed it over and over.

GERALD. I don't know what to say.

HERBERT. You don't have to say anything. Too full
    of emotion, eh?

GERALD. I suppose that's what it is.

HERBERT. Well, You're a very lucky girl, Fiona. He's
    a great little fellow. Straight as a die. Never let you
    down. Now you'll want the ceremony as soon as
    possible. Getting married is like going to the dentist.
    .... it pays to get it over quickly.

GERALD. *(Weakly)* I'm afraid I haven't given it a lot
    of thought.

HERBERT. No need to. That's the province of the
    bride's parents. Tell you what, I'll treat you to a
    special licence so you don't have to wait.

GERALD. I could wait ... *(HERBERT scowls)* .... a
    little while.

HERBERT. Go on with you. A few moments ago you
    couldn't wait. Well, it won't be long now.

PAULINE. *(Dramatically)* Oh, Fiona, I'm so happy I

want to burst out singing.

HERBERT. *(Firmly)* Oh, no you don't.

PAULINE. Let joy be unconfined. *(She bursts into tears).*

FIONA. *(Coming to comfort PAULINE)* I'm happy too. *(She bursts into tears)*

The two women weep and whisper during the next speech, and after a moment or two make their way, with quiet excitement out of the room.

HERBERT. *(His hand on GERALD's shoulder, taking him aside.)* I'm so happy that little talk I had with you earlier did the trick. Bolstered up the old courage, eh? It's only a question of taking the plunge, son, isn't it? Now you've done it everything will be plain sailing.

GERALD. I feel in a bit of a daze. Everything happened so quickly.

HERBERT. It usually does in the end. *(He moves away L. Turns.)* Well, son, you've got yourself a wonderful girl. You realise that, don't you?

GERALD. Oh, yes, Fiona's very ... well, she is a wonderful girl.

HERBERT. Passionate nature. Wonderful cook. Her price is above rubies.

GERALD. *(Still in a daze)* Ruby who?

HERBERT. I mean you've got a real treasure there.

GERALD. *(Recovering from the shock somewhat and seeing a way out)* I know. That's why I'm so worried.

HERBERT. Worried?

GERALD. I don't think I'm worthy of her, Mr. Farson.

HERBERT. Of course you are, Gerald.

GERALD. I'm not much of a catch really, Mr. Farson. I haven't much of a job.

HERBERT. I thought you were a company director.

GERALD. *(Very pleased to admit it)* Oh, I was just pushing a line, I'm afraid. I'm a trainee manager, really. Lowest of the low! My wages hardly cover my insurance. contributions.

HERBERT. Well, what's it matter? Although you'll
find it pretty hard to believe my origins were humble,
you know. It's what a man makes of himself that
counts.

GERALD. I don't think I shall make much of myself...
ever. I've got a grasshopper mind. No determination
at all.

HERBERT. Once you're married you'll buckle down to
things. Be the making of you.

GERALD. I'm a bit of a waster. I drink quite a bit, you
know. Spirits. *(Pause)* Smoke about fifty a day *(Pause*
HERBERT is not impressed.) Inverterate gambler.
(Pause) Never win though. And ... women! Well, there'
been hundreds of them, I'm afraid.

HERBERT. Well, when we're young we all like a fling.
I know. Never thinking of tomorrow. Once you're
married all that will change.

GERALD. I wonder. My mother says I have a basic
instabilityl I think I've got a rather nasty cruel streak,
too.

HERBERT. You're too modest young man. Never under-
estimate yourself. You're going to make a model husband. You see if I'm not right.

GERALD. I wouldn't like you to be disappointed in me.

HERBERT. *(With terrific confidence)* I'm sure I'm not
going to be *(Pause)* Look,You did mean all those lovel
things you were saying to Fiona, about wanting her
and all that? You weren't in my house, alone, with the
doors bolted simply so you could ... well, you know.
You did mean it when you proposed to her?

GERALD. Well, Mr. Farson, to be quite honest with you
the position is that ...

HERBERT. *(Hurriedly)* Of course you were sincere. It
was insulting of me to ask. Forget I ever spoke. *(Pause,*
You know, seeing you on your knees proposing to my
daughter reminded me of a case I know, Friend of
mine. Similar circs. Then the young man let the girl

down. That father sued for every penny that lad had...
and more. That was twenty years ago. Poor chap's still
paying. You take my word for it, Gerald. Marriage in
your case makes economic sense. *(PAULINE and
FIONA enter with the wedding dress left over from
last March. PAULINE holds it up against her daughter
to see the effect. Both women are still crying.)* Oh, cut
it out you two. You don't see Gerald and me crying.
*(But Gerald is almost on the verge of tears. He stands,
a lonely, bewildered figure, D.L.C. his handkerchief
in his hand. Be blows his nose, wipes hiw brow, dabs
his eyes.)* This is a happy occasion and we ought to
celebrate. (At Sideboard R.) Not much here! Just
enough Scotch for one. Well, I suppose father ought
to have it. *(He holds up the glass to give a toast and
sees the forlorn GERALD).* On second thoughts your
need is greater than mine.

*HERBERT crosses with glass to GERALD. Holds it
out for him to take. Without thinking GERALD dips the
hankerchief into the whisky and wipes his brow with
it as*

THE CURTAIN FALLS.

ACT TWO

Scene One. The scene is the same. Several days later.
The morning of the wedding. About eleven o'clock.
The wedding cake stands on the table C. back wall
and presents are on the sideboard and another table
L. The rooms looks untidy. AUNT MELINDA, an
imposing woman, wanders around examining the
presents.

AUNT M. I hope I won't be in the way, Pauline. I
    came early. Thought I might be able to give you a
    hand.
PAULINE. I don't think there's much else to be done.
JENNY. *(Coming from the hall)* Dad says has his
    morning suit arrived yet. He's getting worried he'll
    have nothing to go in.
PAULINE. Oh, there's hours. It'll be here.
AUNT M. Men! They're worse than we are in a crisis.
JENNY..It's not exactly a crisis, auntie. It's a wedding.
    (She goes out. Calls upstairs : 'It hasn't come yet'.)
AUNT M. How's the bride bearing up.
PAULINE. Quite steady. Of course, she's used to this
    sort of thing.
AUNT M. All that fiasco last March! Ever heard what
    happened to that fellow.
PAULINE..Johnny Spinet? No. Disappeared off the fac
    of the earth.
AUNT M. Funny how men's nerves fail them when it
    comes to the crunch.
PAULINE. Quite a few do manage to get to the church.
    Melinda.

AUNT M. Don't try and defend them, Pauline.

PAULINE. Fiona thinks Johnny must have lost his memory or ... been hi-jacked.

AUNT M. Nonsense. He got cold feet and ran for it.

PAULINE. Do you know that if he came back to her she'd throw herself into his arms? All would be forgiven. She told me last night that she still dreams about him.

AUNT M. You can't get into much trouble dreaming. She can go on doing that after she's married. So I suppose she doesn't really love this Gerald.

PAULINE. Oh, yes, she loves him all right. But not in a really tremendous way. Only enough to marry him.

AUNT M. And what about him?

PAULINE. Gerald's crazy ... about her. Oh, yes, quite crazy..

AUNT M. What's this, the cake?

PAULINE. *(Getting annoyed with AUNT M's tone)* No, Melinda, it's a shrunken head ... iced.

AUNT M. No need to be rude. You musn't let your nerves get a hold. What's it made of, anyway? Marble?

PAULINE. Oh, that blue streaky effect. Jenny iced it. I think her fingers were a bit inky.

JENNY. *(Entering from the hall)* Another present's just arrived.. From Mrs. Arbothnot.

PAULINE. Stop trying to see what it is.

JENNY. I know what it is. It's another toast rack.

PAULINE. Oh, no, that makes seven.

JENNY. They can always use them to stack records.

PAULINE..Has Dad fixed the cistern yet?

JENNY. Won't be long. He's up there chewing gum like mad. I'm going to finish off the trifles. *(Exits to kitchen.)*

AUNT M. *(Looking out through french windows)* What's the marquee for? Going to have a circus?

PAULINE. Herbert's idea. For the overspill, he said.

AUNT M. Overspill! Herbert always did have illusions of grandeur.

PAULINE. He's practical, too. He says if beer's going to be spilt it'll do less harm out there on the lawn than in here on the carpet.

AUNT M. I do hope it isn't going to be a rough 'do.'

PAULINE. Oh, no, Herbert wants everything quite genteel. Not like when Ariadne was married.

AUNT M. Well, it was ridiculous to invite the entire rugby team.

PAULINE. The ambulance driver told me that was the first time he'd ever run a shuttle service to a wedding reception.

AUNT M. I'm going to freshen up, Pauline. I've brought something a bit startling to wear to the church. Tell you the truth, I was almost tempted to wear my see-through blouse. *(She goes out almost knocking into JENNY.)*

JENNY. *(Entering from hall)* Another telegram's just come. *(She begins to open it.)*

JENNY. Fiona won't mind. It'll be the usual guff, anyway, 'Congratulations. May all your troubles be little ones,' or 'Get well soon,' or something like that. *(As she reads the telegram her expression changes to one of immense excitement.)* WHOW!

PAULINE. Not from Gerald? He hasn't made a bolt for it.

JENNY. Not from Gerald at all. *(Heading)* 'Hope to be with you this morning. To explain. And be forgiven. Still love you like crazy. Johnny.'

PAULINE. Johnny? Johnny Spinet!

JENNY. I said he'd turn up one day.

PAULINE. You never did. You always reckoned he'd gone into a monastery.

JENNY. Nunnery, dear. A nunnery for Johnny.

PAULINE. Where did it come from?

JENNY. The telegraph boy brought it.

PAULINE. I mean where was it sent from.

JENNY. Whow! It's local. That means he's hovering around somewhere.

PAULINE. Give it to me.

JENNY. What for *(She hands over the telegram.)*

PAULINE. *(Tearing up telegram)* That's what for. Now don't you say a word about this to Fiona.

JENNY. She'd be very pleased. It's terribly romantic. Like a lover coming back from the dead.

PAULINE. This one had better stay dead. At least until after the wedding.

JENNY. But he says he's going to come here.

PAULINE. If that happens we've got to get rid of him ... and without Fiona knowing anything about it. Go and get your father, Jenny. This needs his brains.

JENNY. *(Halting at the doorway, excited)* Wouldn't it be marvellous if he turned up at the church and just as the Vicar asked if anyone knew any reason why these two should not be joined he jumped on his pew and said his piece.

PAULINE. It wouldn't be marvellous at all. It would be tragic.

JENNY. If you ask me this wedding needs livening up a bit. *(She goes out and upstairs.)*

PAULINE tidies around the room ..... at least she moves things from one place to another. She is singing Oh, Happy Wedding Day. She does not hear DEREK's first knock on the french windows.

DEREK. *(Knocking again and getting her attention)* Excuse me. I couldn't make you hear at the front. I think your bell is on the blink.

PAULINE..Oh, yes. My husband is going to mend it. *(Slight Pause)* I know you, don't I? Ah, yes, you're the man who came to mend the cistern, aren't you?

DEREK. No. My name's Derek Colbert. We have met, though on the previous occasion *(With a shy smile)*

I was a bit short on trousers, I'm afraid.

PAULINE. Was it as long ago as that?

DEREK. I'd just like a few words with Jenny ... without Mr. Farson knowing I'm here if that's possible.

JENNY. *(As she enters, not seeing DEREK at first)* Dad can't come. He's got his finger in the hole. *(Sees DEREK)* Oh, Derek! *(Runs to him and greets him with a flamboyant embrace.)*

DEREK. *(Extricating himself)* Hallo, Jenny. Nice to see you.

JENNY. Oh, it's marvellous to see you, Derek. Incredibly marvellous. But where have you been? Why did you walk out on me? Oh, mother, go and make a cup of tea or something.

Automatically PAULINE obeys but gets to the doorway and then, with a bewildered look, turns.

DEREK. I had to take the test film down to Cannes. To show J.A. Then he made me go on to the Venice Festival with him. Sorry I couldn't get in touch with you.

JENNY. *(Very excited)* Oh, what did he say?

DEREK. He wants you.

JENNY. He wants me!

PAULINE. What's that?

JENNY. It's all too technical for you, mother.

PAULINE. *(In a panic as things seem to be beyond her)* I'm going to get your father. He'll have to take his finger out. *(She goes out and upstairs.)*

DEREK. Take his finger out of what?

JENNY. The cistern.

DEREK. Does he keep it in there, then?

JENNY. Never mind about that. Tell me about the film. When do I start.

DEREK. Our lawyers are drawing up a contract right now.

JENNY. I'm so excited I think I'm going to faint.

She pretends to faint, falling back into DEREK's Arms.

DEREK. I seem to have a peculiar effect on this family.

JENNY. *(Recovering from the 'faint' and embracing him)* You have a most peculiar effect on me, Derek.

DEREK. *(Gently pushing her away)* That's bad.

JENNY. No, it isn't. It's wonderful. Do you know every night before I go to sleep I re-live that afternoon on your yacht.

DEREK. Oh, yes.

JENNY. I keep wondering where I went wrong.

DEREK. Wrong? I though you were all right. You satisfied me ... and J.A., too, it seems.

JENNY. But why weren't you ... oh, how shall I put it?

DEREK. You needn't put it at all. I know what you mean. Listen, Jenny, I think you're a wonderful girl ...

JENNY. *(Rapturously)* Oh, do you really?

DEREK. Let me finish ... a wonderful girl and exactly right for the part of Alyse Fontelle. That's all, really.

JENNY. But it can't be all?

DEREK. I don't know what you are thinking about me but whatever it is, I shouldn't I mean, I am married. As a matter of fact, I'm in the process of getting rid of my fourth wife.

JENNY. It isn't true.

DEREK. You're right. it isn't quite true. She is in the process of getting rid of me. I don't blame her. Not one of them could live with me and my obsession.

JENNY. Obsession?

HERBERT enters. Followed by PAULINE who looks distinctly worried.

HERBERT. *(Storming in)* I thought I'd made it clear to you, Mr. Seducer, that if you showed your face in this house again ...

DEREK. I'm just going. I only came with a message for Jenny.

JENNY. About my film test, Daddy, Wonderful news!

HERBERT. Film test? When?

DEREK. Oh, didn't you know? One afternoon a little while ago. On my yacht. I thought Jenny would have told you.

JENNY. No. I didn't think you'd understand, Daddy.

HERBERT. You're right. I don't. On this fellow's yacht What am I going to hear next?

What he hears next is the VICAR singing 'You'll never walk alone' as he comes in through the french windows.

VICAR. Ah, happy, happy people. I couldn't make myself heard at the front. I think your bell's playing up.

HERBERT. I know, Vicar, I'm going to fix it as soon as I've got a second to spare.

VICAR. *(To DEREK)* Do I know you?

JENNY. You ought to, Vicar, You of all people.

VICAR. *(Troubled that he has forgotten something again)* Oh, yes, of course. You are the groom, are you not?

JENNY. It's Derek Colbert, the great film director.

PAULINE indicates that VICAR should sit near her, in chair left, and he crosses and sits.

HERBERT. That's his story. I wonder anyone's got the cheek to use it any more. To tell you the truth, Vicar, you saved this fellow's bacon walking in when you did.

VICAR. It does go off very quickly this hot weather. Mrs. Throgmorton's always complaining.

HERBERT. *(Giving him a look)* Well, she's got good cause to. *(To DEREK)* You! Get!

DEREK. I'll be back, Jenny.

HERBERT. Get out of here before I .....

PAULINE. Manners, Herbert, manners. *(To DEREK, earnestly)* Get going, you fool.

DEREK. Perhaps you're right. See you this afternoon, Jenny. *(Exits to garden.)*

HERBERT. *(In a rage at french windows)* You will not see my daughter ... not now ... not ever ...*(Screaming)* NEVER!

JENNY. *(Whimpering)* How dare you treat him like that? An artist! He's so sensitive. People shouldn't shout at him. Beauty means nothing to you.

HERBERT. *(With an exaggerated sigh)* Oh, my gawd!

VICAR. I think your father must my dear, or he would not have married your dear mother.

PAULINE..Oh, Vicar. What a kind ... and truthful man you are!

JENNY. I didn't mean that kind of beauty. That kind fades.

HERBERT. *(Mumbling)* Your telling me.

JENNY. I was talking about beauty of the spirit.

HERBERT. *(Showing her his clenched fist)* I know one thing my girl. If he comes here again I shall give him a beauty.

JENNY. *(Exasperated)* Philistines! *(She flounces out of the room)*

VICAR. I really must reproach you, Mr. Farson, for your aggressive attitude towards that young man. He who lives by the sword shall perish by the sword.

HERBERT. *(Coming to C.)* It's not exactly living by the sword to tell him to keep away from my daughter. You mustn't imagine, Vicar, that everyone is as straight forward and upright as you and me. This world is peopled, by a pretty evil and vicious crows. *(THE VICAR raises a hand in denial of this)* Oh, yes. If it wasn't you'd be out of a job.

PAULINE. You're a very hard man, Herbert. You set such high standards .... for others.

VICAR. Now, come. We mustn't quarrel on this happy morning. I called round, Mrs. Farson, because I have been awake all night.

PAULINE. *(With a little laugh)* Not conscience, I hope.

VICAR. Yes, quite conscious and worried, too. I got out

of bed a half-dozen times and tried it. But to no avail.
I think I need your expert touch. That's why I came
round here.

HERBERT. Well, my wife hasn't must time for touching t
morning, Vicar. We have got a wedding on our hands fo
this afternoon, you know.

VICAR. I'm not likely to forget that. am I?

*But the glances PAULINE and HERBERT
exchange above the VICAR's head signify that
they are not so sure. There is a pause.*

PAULINE. If you'd be kind enough to wait, Vicar ...
outside perhaps. I have something very important
to say to my husband.

*She takes VICAR's arm and leads him towards
garden.*

HERBERT. If it's more money you're after, Pauline,
let me tell you now you haven't an earthly. This
'do's' already costing me next week's benefit.

PAULINE. It's not about money. Much more important
than that.

HERBERT. Gerald? He's shot himself!

PAULINE. If you wouldn't mind, Vicar, Why not sit in
the tent .... and ... and amuse yourself? I won't forget
you're there.

VICAR. I don't suppose I shall, either. *(He goes out)*

HERBERT. Now, what are you bursting a blood vessel
over?

PAULINE. Someone's coming here today who could
throw a spanner in the works.

HERBERT. Spanner! Oh, that reminds me. I've had to
turn off the cistern.

PAULINE. this is serious. Herbert. Johnny Spinet's
back in town.

HERBERT. *(Bristling exaggeratedly)* Where is he? I'll
flay him alive.

PAULINE. No need for that now, Herbert.

HERBERT. He wronged my Fiona, didn't he?

PAULINE. He might have wronged her. But at three
o'clock this afternoon she's being righted. All that
matters is that he doesn't walk in here just before
Fiona leaves for the Church and cause an ... an
emotional earthquake.

HERBERT. I shall be causing the earthquake.

PAULINE. You'll do nothing of the sort. What you
don't realise, expert on human nature though you say
you are, is that Fiona still wants that boy.

HERBERT. After humiliating her before one of the
biggest congregations St. George's had for years!
I can't believe it.

PAULINE. Fiona likes Gerald all right and she'll
make him a good wife, but when you speak about over-
whelming passion ...

HERBERT. I very seldom do.

PAULINE. Then's it's Johnny Spinet.

HERBERT. Oh, the infamy of women! I don't think
any man could be that two-faced.

PAULINE. Men are two faced, too. He's sent a telegram
saying that he can explain missing the wedding in
March and that he still loves her.

HERBERT. That's all very well. But would he marry
her. Oh, no, he's too much of a fly-by-night ... and
a fly-by-day, too.

PAULINE. I thought I ought to tell you.

HERBERT. You did right for once, mother. Now what
we must do is give him the cold shoulder.

*Enter FIONA in hair curlers in a net and wearing
dressing gown.*

FIONA. Dad, What have you done to the bathroom?

PAULINE. Oh, Herbert, you haven't been careless again?

FIONA. I can't get any hot water.

HERBERT. Well, you won't. I've turned the cistern
off.

FIONA. You can't do that.

HERBERT. It's either that or standing up there all day

with my finger in the hole.

FIONA. But I want a hot bath.

HERBERT. You'll have to have a cold bath, won't you?
It'll cool your ardour. Either that or do without one.

PAULINE. You can't send her unwashed to her bridal bed

HERBERT, Well, use your brains. You're going on your
honeymoon. Have one at the hotel.

FIONA. I won't get a chance. Not with Gerald.

HERBERT. Well, I can't turn it on again. Not unless
we're prepared to issue all the guests with waders.

FIONA. Oh, what a house! *(She flounces out to hall
and upstairs.)*

HERBERT. Would you believe it? The ingratitude! And
look at the money I've spent on beer.

PAULINE. Be patient with her, Herbert. After all she
doesn't get married every day.

PAULINE. Anyway, nothing is so pressing as this
problem of Johnny Spinet.

HERBERT. You leave that one to me mother.

PAULINE. It's no use you thinking you can head him off
by knocking his head off.

HERBERT. I've abandoned that plan. I'll be more subtle.
I've got to think up some story to get him out of town
again.

JENNY. *(Entering with a parcel)* This looks like it.

PAULINE. Oh, yes, it does, doesn't it?

HERBERT. What?

PAULINE. Your morning suit, dear.

HERBERT. *(Boyishly pleased)* Oh, good. I'll go and
try it on. I pay for dressing, you know, and this is a
good opportunity to show off my figure. *(He takes
the parcel and goes out to hall.)*

JENNY. I've finished the trifles. Are they supposed to
be dark bottle-green?

PAULINE. What did you use?

JENNY. Raspberries.

PAULINE. *(Who can't be bothered any more with details*

I should think they'd be all right, dear.

JENNY. I shall have to get ready soon. As soon as the sausage rolls are done.

PAULINE. Good gracious, look at the time. I've got an appointment with Maurice at eleven. He wants to do something extraordinary with me.

AUNT M. *Entering from hall, wearing a sort of Carmen Miranda hat)* Pauline, I'm worried about my hat. Tell me it's all right.

PAULINE. *(Automatically without thinking)* It's all right.

AUNT M. No, look at it. I bought it yesterday.' especially. It's not too way out, is it?

JENNY. This wedding's got everything, auntie. There's no reason why it shouldn't have your hat.*(She goes out to hall.)*

AUNT M. One does like to strike the right note.

PAULINE. I don't understand you, Melinda. You enjoy a wedding and yet you dislike men.

AUNT M. Yes, I must admit I do get a kick out of a wedding. The cooky young man shyly answers, 'I do' and he's cooked his goose for the rest of his life. It's rather like sitting by the guillotine.

PAULINE. *(Acidly)* Why don't you take your knitting, then?

AUNT M. If the wait we had last March is anything to go by I'll have time to run myself up a cardigan.

PAULINE. There's not going to be any hitch this time.

HERBERT. *(Enters wearing the morning coat which is much too small for him)* Look at this thing! What do they think I am, a midget.

PAULINE. Oh, my!

HERBERT. When you ordered it you did give my measurements and not yours.

PAULINE. You're just not used to it. You'll look fine.

AUNT M. *(With a sly smile)* Um, you're going to cut quite a figure, Herbie

HERBERT. Yes, a figure of fun.

PAULINE. It looks wrong because of the way you're standing.

HERBERT. *(Exasperated)* What, upright? I'm supposed to be down on all fours, am I? *(He makes half an attempt to get on his knees.)*

PAULINE. *(Dragging up)* Oh, don't be silly. But you're sticking your arms out.

HERBERT. *(With leaden sarcasm)* Aren't they supposed to come out of the bottom then.

PAULINE. Yes, but not so much. Pull them back. *(He pulls his arms up in his sleeves a bit)* A bit more. *(He does so)* That's better. Now a litte bit more.

HERBERT. *(Relaxing)* If I pull them up any more I'll dislocate my shoulder.

PAULINE. Oh, well, you'll simply have to wear a shirt with plenty of cuff.

HERBERT. I'm going to look like one of those characters in Mad Movies.

AUNT M. You're just not used to such elegance, Herbie.

HERBERT. Don't try and smarm me. *(Turning on PAULINE)* I'm not sure you didn't do this on purpose, Pauline. I've a damned good mind to go in khaki shorts and a bush jacket.

PAULINE. For years I've tried to get you to look a bit smarter. Now you've got the opportunity you're complaining.

HERBERT. *(Throwing his handkerchief over his crooked arm, like a waiter)* At least, I might pick up a few tips. *(He goes out in a huff)*.

PAULINE. Oh, that man! Sometimes I feel like screaming.

AUNT M. Then scream, my dear, and relieve yourself.

PAULINE is about to scream. Then she collects herself. JENNY enters shyly from the kitchen.

JENNY. Mum, don't be angry. I forgot the sausage rolls. *(Pause, with downcast eyes)* I've burnt them. *(Pause, almost in tears)* All eighty.

PAULINE *(In a hushed voice)* Very bad?

JENNY. Black!

PAULINE. *(Looks wildly about her, wondering what's to be done; then:)* Oh, well, you'd better chip off the pastry and stick the sausages on sticks.

JENNY. I think there's someone banging at the front door.

Glad of the opportunity, JENNY escapes to answer the door.

PAULINE. Could be Johnny Spinet. I'll have to get Herbert to deal with him. *(She goes out)*

IVY. *(Appearing in the archway after a few monents)* In here?

JENNY. *(Off)* That's right.

RONALD enters. He is followed by GERALD. JENNY bringing up the rear, IVY and RONALD both show great distaste for the surroundings. GERALD has the appearance of a whipped puppy.

JENNY. Oh, has Mum gone? Well, this is my Aunt Melinda, Auntie this is *(Suddenly remembering in panic)* ... I've got three pints of milk on the stove *(Dashes out to kitchen.)*

AUNT M. Hello, Gerald.

GERALD. Aunt Melinda, this is my mother and father. Just arrived. They want to meet Fiona's people before the wedding.

AUNT M. Oh, they will be pleased to see you. Won't you sit down.

IVY flicks chair with her handkerchief and then sits D.L. RONALD sits on settee. Then leaps up.

AUNT M. Good gracious, another toast rack.

RONALD. *(Handing the toast rack to AUNT M.)* I thought for a moment it was a mouse-trap.

AUNT M. *(Takes toast rack, puts it with the other*

presents on sideboard and then sits again R.) You're
a naughty boy, Gerald, coming here this morning.
Don't you know it's unlucky to see the bride before the
wedding.

RONALD. Sometimes it's just as unlucky to see her
afterwards.

IVY. Ronald, try and confine your remarks to essentials.
Gerald hasn't come to see the Bride. Nothing is
further from his mind.

GERALD. I wouldn't mind a little peek.

IVY. *(Firmly)* Gerald, contain yourself. *(To AUNT M.)*
Mr. and Mrs. Farson know we're here?

AUNT M. Don't worry. News travels fast in this house.
. *(Pause, making conversation)* Mr. Farson's trying on
his morning suit. He's so excited. He's been looking
forward to this day for so long. *(No answer. A long
silence. Then, to RONALD.)* I know you, don't I?

RONALD. *(Haughtily)* I think that very unlikely, madam.

AUNT M. I'm sure I've seen you somewhere before.

IVY. His photograph, perhaps, in one of the more
fashionable monthlies. Since he married me my
husband has been quite well known.

RONALD. Very well, I should say dear,

IVY. In certain circles, yes.

AUNT M. I don't know much about those circles. I'm a
bit of a square myself. *(There is a long silence.
AUNT M. finally gets restive and rises).* Well, would
you excuse me?

IVY. *(Beaming with joy)* With the greatest of pleasure.

AUNT M. I'm helping the bride to get into her dress
She's going to look absolutely ravishing. Have you
told your parents how lucky you are, young man?
(She goes out.)

RONALD. *(Glaring at GERALD with contempt.)* Lucky.

IVY. The incredible thing is, she meant it.

RONALD. *(Rising angry)* If only you'd wired us sooner
we could have come home to help you out of this.

(By french windows) What's that tent doing out there?

GERALD. *(Looking from C.)* It's not doing anything. Just standing.

RONALD. I wouldn't be surprised if they didn't live in it.

IVY. More likely they keep the goats in it, dear.

RONALD. *(Coming to C.)* How in God's name did you get involved in this?

IVY. Didn't it once occur to you, Gerald, in these transports of infatuation that you had a social position to keep up? Your father never married for love.

RONALD. *(Mumbling)* I didn't know that at the time.

GERALD. *(Sitting in the chair)* Aren't you jumping to conclusions? You haven't met Fiona yet.

IVY. Oh, really, Gerald. One has only to look around one.

GERALD. It's bound to be a bit untidy on the morning of a wedding.

IVY. God knows what their bedrooms are like.

GERALD. Oh, they're quite ... *(Remembers himself)* quite ordinary I should think.

IVY. And who is that awful woman with the Carmen Miranda hat that we've just been entertained by?

GERALD. Oh, that's Aunt Melinda. She's a good sort.

IVY. A good sort of what, I'd like to know. The cheek, to say she knew your father!

RONALD. *(Hurriedly changing the subject)* You used to choose such sophisticated friends. We go off to Bermuda for a couple of months and you're hobnobbing with the hoipoloi.

GERALD. Doing what?

RONALD. Hobnobbing with the hoiopoi. Oh, you know what I mean.

IVY. I can only suppose they're after your money.

GERALD. I've never told them I had any. I said I was a trainee manager at Fair Deal Stores. I never said you owned them.

IVY. Oh, these people have second sight.

HERBERT. *(Entering breezily)* Ah, good morning all.

GERALD. *(Attemping to rise from his chair)* Good morning, Mr. Farson..

HERBERT. *(Pushing him back into his chair)* It is a good morning indeed, my son. Did you hear that? My son! Came out quite naturally, didn't it?

GERALD. Mr. Farson, I'd like you to .....

HERBERT. No, no. Not Mr. Farson any longer, lad. Call me Dad.

GERALD. Oh, all right. Well, Dad, I'd like you to meet mother.

HERBERT. Your mother. And father? Well, isn't that fine. But you told me they were in Bermondsey .... or somewhere.

IVY. Bermuda.

HERBERT. Oh, well, I knew it was some nig-nog place. *(Crosses to IVY)* Well, how are you? *(He shakes hands with her)* I'm so glad you could be in at the death .... in a manner of speaking.

IVY. Charmed, I'm sure.

HERBERT. *(To RONALD)* I'm pleased to meet you Mr. Dunjon. Now what line would you be in? No, don't tell me. *(Sizing him up)* You wouldn't be in the undertaking business.

RONALD. *(Most offended)* Not if I could help it.

HERBERT. Oh, well, never mind.

GERALD. I thought it was right to introduce you rather than have you meet as strangers at the church.

HERBERT. You're quite right, son. Well, this is the moment I've been waiting for. I'm not saying it's the moment Gerald's been waiting for. That's a few hours off yet, isn't it, son?

IVY. Such talk! Is nothing sacred?

HERBERT. Oh, don't mind me. Everyone says I'm a bit of a wit. I'll be having you laugh your head off before the day's out, you see if I don't. By the way, do you like pickled onions.

IVY. I can't say that I've ever seen one.

HERBERT. Then I've got a treat in store for you. A massive jar of them out there in the tent. Washed down with a beaker of champagne .... lovely!

PAULINE. *(As she enters)* Sorry to have kept you so long in attendance.

HERBERT. Gerry's Mum and and Dad, dear. Just dropped in to say good luck.

PAULINE. *(Extending a tentative hand to RONALD)* How nice to meet you.

RONALD. *(Reluctantly taking PAULINE's hand to shake)* How do you do?

PAULINE. I'm quite all right. *(She turns to IVY whose presence overawes her)* And Mrs. ....*(She drops a little courtesy.)*

IVY. Now I can't disguise the fact that this business has been a shock to us. A surprise, anyway. We didn't know a thing about this wedding until yesterday. We were in Bermuda and when Gerald's cable came we flew home at once. We only arrived this morning.

PAULINE. Oh, Gerry, lovely surprises. Remember the night he proposed, Herbert?

HERBERT. Not half!

PAULINE. By sheer chance we came into this room and there he was on his hands and knees begging our Fiona to marry him.

HERBERT. We had no idea it was in the air.

IVY. It's hard to understand. Gerald has always consulted me about anything of importance. Had you been drinking?

GERALD. Only water.

HERBERT. Ah, yes, it was the water that did it.

IVY. It would have been better to have waited, I'm sure.

HERBERT. Well, he couldn't.

IVY. Couldn't?

HERBERT. He was dead scared someone was going to

jump in and get her before he did. That's why he had to move so fast. Right, son?

GERALD. Well ... I ... wasn't all that fast ... I ...

HERBERT. I don't know. If you'd been any faster you'd have been away on your honeymoon by now.

RONALD. *(Standing)* Mr. Farson. Mrs. Farson. I have a proposal to make to you.

HERBERT Aye, Aye, what's this? Proposing to my wife.

RONALD. *(Confused)* I did not mean that sort of proposal Mr. Farson.

HERBERT. Only joking, old boy. Got to get used to a few jokes in this house. Gerald'll tell you. *(GERALD nods)*.

RONALD. My proposition is that the wedding be postpone

HERBERT. *(Shocked)* Postponed? You mean, put off?

PAULINE. Oh, no, I couldn't face that. *(On the verge of breaking)*

HERBERT. Now, don't talk daft. How can it be postponed I've got the beer in and the place is littered with toast racks.

RONALD. I'm not saying that it wouldn't be embarrassing But better be unhappy for one day than miserable for the rest of your life.

HERBERT. Who are you talking about?

RONALD. Your daughter, of course.

HERBERT. Oh, she won't be miserable. She'll make the best of things even if there is something wrong with your boy.

IVY. *(Bristling)* There's nothing wrong with Gerald.

GERALD. *(Offended)* No, there's nothing wrong with me.

IVY. *(To GERALD)* You talk too much. That's been your undoing.

RONALD. Nothing wrong except that he has deceived you

PAULINE. *(A touch of panic)* He's married already. I knew it. I felt some evil force lurking in the corner.

HERBERT. No, you can't pull that one. He's not married. I checked.

RONALD. And the reason he isn't married is that he's

never been able to afford it. He couldn't support a wife.

HERBERT. Wife ... and family.

IVY. *(Aghast)* What? You mean your daughter is going to..

HERBERT. *(Although he didn't mean this HERBERT seizes on to the idea.)* Wouldn't be a bit surprised ... the way he used to carry on. Remember that night, dear, just before he proposed ... the way we saw him dancing around this room. What did I say to you? I said, 'That's an African fertility dance, If ever I've seen one.'

GERALD. *(Weakly)* I had cramp.

HERBERT. A likely story.

RONALD. I repeat. He is unable to support a wife. He is only a trainee manager, you know. Sort of apprentice.

HERBERT. At the moment, yes. But that boy's got prospects. If I guess right, one day He's going to be Managing Director of your stores.

RONALD. All right. Let's leave this marriage idea until he is Managing Director, shall we?

IVY. *(Rising)* Let me be brutally frank.

GERALD. No mother. Don't.

IVY. Yes. It appears to us ... and it would so appear to any normal, unbiased person ... that advantage has been taken of my son.

HERBERT. Oh, don't give me that. He's not a babe in arms.

IVY. As far as girls are concerned, he is.

PAULINE. That's not what Fiona says. She says he wants quite a bit of handling.

IVY. I don't doubt that my son is healthy. But I wasn't speaking about the physical side.

RONALD. You never do.

IVY. *(Ignoring RONALD)* Psychologically he's naive. When we arrived at his flat this morning he was lying on his bed in tears. 'Am I doing right, mummy? he kept whimpering. Naturally I was worried.

HERBERT. No need. Every young man is like that on the

morning of his wedding.

IVY. *(Surprised by this news)* You weren't, were you, Ronald?

RONALD. You know, my dear, how overjoyed I was. I was round at the church as soon as they opened.

IVY. Exactly, and if this had been a genuine love-match Gerald would have been up with the lark, smothering himself in after-shave and smoking innumerable cigarettes.

GERALD. I don't smoke.

IVY. Be quiet. You talk too much. I think the right and proper thing to do is to give Gerald the opportunity of recanting.

HERBERT. Here, just a minute. You know you've got a hell of a cheek. Coming here, an hour or two, before the wedding, with my darling girl upstairs there now making herself more lovely than ever for this special occasion ... and now you propose to ask him ... him ... if she may be permitted to be married. I've never in all my life ...

IVY. It's for the best. I propose to ask Gerald if he would not be happier if this wedding were postponed.

RONALD. When he has answered I hope your conscience will cause you to think again.

HERBERT sums up the position, glancing at GERALD who sits open—mouthed and gormless in his chair.

HERBERT. Okay, Okay, ask him. I'll be bound by the answer he gives provided you are, too.

RONALD. *(Surprised)* You don't mind?

HERBERT. Ask him anything you like. He's your son.

IVY. He's my son, actually.

RONALD. I must say that's very civil of you, Mr. Farson Directly I caught sight of you I said to Ivy, 'This man is a gentleman. He'll see reason.'

IVY. *(Surprised)* Did you?

RONALD. *(Giving her a nudge)* You know I did.

IVY. Oh, yes.

HERBERT. *(Proudly)* I should have thought that went without saying.

PAULINE. I don't know. I've always found that when a gentleman calls you a gentleman he means you're not a gentleman at all.

HERBERT. *(Giving PAULINE a long doubting look)* You know dear, it's a pity you packed in those Logic classes at the Community Centre.

RONALD. The point is are we both going to be bound by his answer.

HERBERT. Provided he understands the nature of the question.

RONALD. *(Sharply)* He's not a half-wit, Mr. Farson.

HERBERT looks doubtfully at the open—mouthed GERALD. IVY crosses and with her hand under his chin, closes his mouth.

HERBERT. No, of course, he's not. And I've already spoken to him of the responsibilities of marriage.

IVY. But not this morning.

HERBERT. No, but a little while ago I told him marriage was a serious business. Didn't I, son?

GERALD. You did say something like that, Mr. Farson.

HERBERT. *(Correcting him)* Dad.

GERALD. Of course, Dad.

IVY. *(Correcting him)* Mr. Farson.

GERALD. *(Not knowing who to please next)* Mr. Farson.

HERBERT. I'm sure he took it all in. Especially the money side. I did explain about the money side, didn't I?

GERALD. Yes. Twenty years to pay.

IVY. Twenty years! What does that mean?

HERBERT. A little story I told your boy. About a young chap who let a girl down. Seemed easy enough at the time. But afterwards he came to regret it. Every Friday afternoon for the next twenty years, he regretted it.

Quite disfigured with grief he was.

IVY. That's beside the point. Now, Gerald, answer your mother truthfully as you did this morning at the flat. Don't you think it would be better if this wedding were postponed for a while? I won't say indefinitely Let's say for ten years or so.

Silence. HERBERT's glare makes GERALD
hesitant.

RONALD. Well, come on, son. It's your future we're thinking of.

HERBERT. Yeh! Me, too.

GERALD. *(At last)* I ... I ... don't quite know what to say ....

IVY. Simply say what you told us this morning when we arrived.

HERBERT. That's right. Speak up, Gerald. No need to be embarrassed. If you've been monkeying around with my daughter, if you promised her marriage just so you could ... well, you know ... Good Lord, I shall understand, son. I've always made it clear that you're a free agent. Do what you think's best for you. You know how I feel about men who have their fling with a girl and then walk off without so much as a Thank You. But ... don't let that affect your answer, son.

GERALD. *(Caves in under HERBERT's menace)* I think ... on the whole ... I think I'd rather go through with it, mum.

IVY. *(Appalled)* You've been drugged or something. Brainwashed.

RONALD. Now you listen to me. I'm just about fed up with your weak-kneed attitude. That's what's got you into all this trouble. If you go through with this marriage against my wishes I'll cut you off without a penny, I'll chuck you out of your job and as far as I'm concerned you can beg for your bread on the street.

IVY. Oh, no, he won't.

RONALD. What?

IVY. It may be the name of your old company on the facia boards, Ronald. But don't forget that I bought you out when you were bankrupt. There's no money of yours in the store. Only mine. And I'm not having any son made destitute. Even if he is an idiot. No matter what he's done or what he intends to do, he's my son. And I shall see he's all right.

RONALD. But it was you who was so upset.

IVY. I might be upset. I wish that things had turned out differently but I've set my mind on Gerald being head of the firm one day. And nothing is more important than that.

GERALD. Good for you, mother.

IVY. Keep quiet, you! It seems to me that we shall all have to make the best of things. So let the wedding take place.

HERBERT. *(With heavy sarcasm)* Oh, that is nice of you. I must nip up and tell Fiona. It's still on. She will be pleased to know that.

IVY. *(Sweeping towards exit)* No need to be sarcastic. Come, Ronald. Come, Gerald. *(IVY and RONALD go out.)*

PAULINE. See you at the church, then.

HERBERT. *(Holding GERALD back)* Glad you stuck up for yourself, son. If you hadn't I'd have called it off myself. *(GERALD looks completely baffled. IVY calls from the hall, 'Come on, Gerald, will you?' And he exits.)* I didn't realise they were going to be such gentry, Pauline. They won't care for beer. I think I'd better nip down to the off-licence and get a half-bottle of British Sherry.

JOHNNY. *(Entering, a little abashed)* Hello, folks!

PAULINE. Johnny!

JOHNNY. Some people were going out. They let me in.

HERBERT. Good God, how you've got the gall to

come back to this house after all the misery you caused
me. I ought to flay you alive, young man.

JOHNNY. I hope you don't.

PAULINE. No, Herbert. You promised not to do that.
Remember?

HERBERT. *(Reluctant to abandon force)* Oh, yes. Well,
what do you want here, anyway?

JOHNNY. I want to see Fiona. I want to explain what
happened to me.

HERBERT. Have you got any idea what happened to her

JOHNNY. I'm not heartless, Mr. Farson. I can imagine
how she felt that day. But she must have known deep
down inside her, that I'd never let her down. Not
willingly.

HERBERT. I don't know about deep inside her. She
looked pretty rough on the outside.

JOHNNY. I've got to have the chance to make amends.
Mr. Farson. *(Seeing the wedding cake)* Hello, someone
getting married?

PAULINE, *(In a panic, doesn't quite know how to handle
this)* Yes.

HERBERT. Yes, that's right. Young Jenny.

JOHNNY. Jenny? Surprise, isn't it?

PAULINE. Quite a surprise. It happened very quickly.

JOHNNY. Must have done. When is it, today? *(PAULINE
bewildered, nods)* Oh, great. I'll go along to the church
and pay my respects.

PAULINE. No, you can't do that.

JOHNNY. Why not? A church is a public place.

HERBERT. Not this one. *(Inventing something)* It's
being held in camera.

JOHNNY. Camera. I didn't know they did that for
weddings.

PAULINE. It's because she's so young.

JOHNNY. Oh, I see. *(Pause)* Well, tell Fiona I'm here, wil
you? I know how you feel about me but when you kno
the whole story you'll think differently. But I must tel

Fiona first.

JENNY. *(Enters)* Mum, what causes custard to go grey? Oh, Johnny! It's good to see you.

PAULINE. Go back to your ... custard, dear.

JOHNNY. Not before I've congratulated you.

JENNY. Thanks. But who told you?

JOHNNY. Your folks of course. I hope it turns out one hundred percent.

JENNY. I'm lucky to get the chance.

JOHNNY. You're a little bit young but ... well,, they told me about it being in camera.

JENNY. *(A little puzzled but ...)* Oh, yes. I had to take a test, of course.

JOHNNY. Test.

JENNY. You couldn't expect him to take me on without a test. I mean, I haven't got any experience. But he's going to tell me exactly what to do.

JOHNNY. Do I know the man?

JENNY. The man? Modigliani, you mean? You might have heard of him. I admire him so much. Apart from painting he must have had about two hundred beautiful women in his life.

JOHNNY. Oh, I didn't think you'd go for that sort.

PAULINE. *(Who with HERBERT, has been watching with bated breath, afraid that JENNY might give the game away)* Now back to the custard, Jenny, dear.

JENNY. Okay. Oh, you'll be able to see the bit with me in bed when it comes on Television. *(She goes out)*

JOHNNY. *(Stares after her, concluding there is something wrong with her mind)* Is she ... all right?

HERBERT. *(Seizing on the idea)* She's not as bad as Fiona.

JOHNNY. What's happened to her? Tell me what's happened.

PAULINE. You tell him.

HERBERT. Me?

PAULINE. Yes, you. You know more about it than I do.

HERBERT. I don't think anyone knows a lot.

JOHNNY. Come on, out with it. I want to know. Is she
  ill? *(He moves towards hall)* Is she lying up there?

HERBERT. *(Holding him back)* No. She's not here at all.

JOHNNY. Not here! Where, then?

HERBERT. Leatherhead.

JOHNNY. Leatherhead? What's she doing in Leatherhead

HERBERT. You don't seem to realise how that ordeal in
  March affected her.

PAULINE. She had to be confined in Leatherhead.

JOHNNY. Confined. So it wasn't a false alarm, then? But
  couldn't you have found somewhere nearer. It's fifty
  miles away.

HERBERT. We didn't mean that sort of confined. She ha
  a breakdown. If you want to see her you'll find her in
  the ... the Hospital for ... for Nervous Women ... in
  Leatherhead.

PAULINE. *(All at sea, feeling she must say something)* W
  visit her every Wednesday and Sunday and .. take her
  jelly babies.

HERBERT. *(Finding it difficult to follow this inconsequ*
  tial remark) She doesn't eat them. Just plays with ther
  Talks to them. She calls everyone: 'My Johnny'.

PAULINE. Even the black ones.

JOHNNY. *(Appalled)* And I drove her to that?

HERBERT. 'Fraid so. Still, you might be able to do some
  thing for her if ...

JOHNNY. Don't worry, I'm going to. I've got my car
  outside. I'll be up there in an hour.

HERBERT. That means you'll be back in two. Oh, no,
  that won't do.

JOHNNY. Why not? I'm not going to hang about.

PAULINE. It's a terribly dangerous road. You want to
  arrive in one piece, don't you? Fiona will expect that.

HERBERT. Don't be foolhardy, son. After all, she's
  been waiting for you since last March. She can wait
  another couple of hours. A steady fifteen miles an hou
  eh?

JOHNNY. I'll see. Is this hospital easy to find?

HERBERT. You might have to ask one or two people. But don't give up till you find it.

JOHNNY. Don't you worry, I won't. Not if it takes all day. *(He dashes out)*

HERBERT. Let's hope it does.

PAULINE. Oh, Herbert, I never thought getting Fiona married would be such a touch and go affair.

HERBERT. Well, he's out of the way for a few hours. By the time he gets back it'll be too late for him to gum up the works.

PAULINE. There isn't any doubt about Gerald turning up?

HERBERT. Oh, no. I'm not making the mistake I made with that fellow who just left here. You know Dodger Weems. He was my runner in the days when I had the book.

PAULINE. Little man in a greasy overcoat? Had a peculiar smell?

HERBERT. That's Dodger. Well, I'm paying him a few quid to keep a day and night watch on young Gerald's flat. This one's not going to get away.

PAULINE. I'll feel happier in my mind when it's all over. Oh, my goodness, the Vicar!

HERBERT. What about him?

PAULINE. Half an hour ago I left him out in the tent. *(Hurries out through french windows and after a moment or two returns in a panic.)* He's gone.

HERBERT. He must be around the house somewhere. Vicars just don't disappear. This isn't your Paul Temple, you know. I'll look up in the back bedroom.

PAULINE. Surely you don't think he's up to your tricks.

HERBERT. I'll have a look just in case. *(He goes out and upstairs)*

PAULINE. *(Looks about her wildly, and then goes to french windows and looks into garden)* Vicar! *(Then she sees him.)* Vicar! Vicar, really! Come away from that fence.

CURTAIN.

WILL YOU TAKE THIS WOMAN

*Scene Two. The Same. A few hours later. A few minutes
before the bride is due to leave for the church.
FIONA, in her wedding dress, paces nervously up and
down. JENNY enters.*

JENNY. Did I leave my nail varnish down here?

FIONA. *(Snappily)* I didn't know you had any.

JENNY. Well, your nail varnish, then.

FIONA. I'm not standing here looking for nail varnish,
am I?

JENNY. Temper! Temper!

FIONA. Well, don't come down here asking such silly
questions.

JENNY. It was rotten nail varnish, anyway. *(Runs out and
upstairs.)*

AUNT M. *(Enters from the hall)* Do you know someone
has turned the cistern off? Of all the stupid things. I
couldn't get any hot water.

FIONA. You can get some in the kitchen.

AUNT M. Oh, it's all right, dear. I had a bit of a struggle
but I turned it on again. *(Slight pause)* You're
feeling a bit nervous, I expect. There's really no need ...
not for the woman.

FIONA. My butterflies have got butterflies. I can't
imagine how poor Gerald must be feeling. He's so
nervous well, in company he is.

AUNT M. Men can't stand pain like we women can. Do you
know much about men?

FIONA. What a question? Well, I suppose you could say
I've got my A-levels.

AUNT M. In my job you've got to know them through and through. Otherwise you'd soon find yourself in trouble.

FIONA. Your job? I never knew you had a job. I thought Uncle Rupert left you well off.

AUNT M. Well, you've got to find something to·do, something to occupy your talents. I do a little part-time work for a detective agency. I don't advertise it. Confidential sort of work.

FIONA. Tracking down spies ... and that sort of thing.

AUNT M. No. I'm more on what you might call the judicial side. Divorce. I'm the woman that the husband is found in the hotel bedroom with.

FIONA. *(Disappointed and a little disgusted)* Oh, no!

AUNT M. Nothing improper in it. Oh, no. I wouldn't stand for that. You just sit there in bed in your nightie and the husband sits there in his nightie ... I mean, his pyjamas. Then at twelve o'clock the detective comes in and takes a photo. Then you all go home. Later you read about the case in the paper.

FIONA. Oh, how terrible!

AUNT M. You don't get mentioned by name. 'Spent the night at such-and-such an hotel with an unknown woman'. That's all. The law requires it. And we supply it.

FIONA. I suppose you would get to know a lot about men in a job like that.

AUNT M. Well, I've done a lot of observing and I've done a lot of thinking and I'm convinced that women are one step higher up the ladder of evolution than men are. Men are still animals really. And when we marry we domesticate them.

FIONA. Do you think Gerald's an animal, then?

AUNT M. They all are. And that's why, if you could see him at the moment, you'd find him in an awful lather. Because he sees the cage in front of him. This after-noon at three o'clock the door snaps shut. From then onwards you're his trainer.

FIONA. I don't think that's a very romantic way of looking at it, auntie.

AUNT M. There's nothing romantic about it. Unless you love animals. It's marriage, facing the facts.

JENNY. *(Entering with toast-rack)* This has just come, from Mrs. Fakenham.

FIONA. *(Terribly disappointed)* Oh, no! Another toast-rack! That makes nine.

JENNY. *(Brightly)* When you get a dozen, if you send them in, you'll get a free packet of corn-flakes. *(She hurries off.)*

FIONA. How much longer?

AUNT M. Your mother, Jenny and I will be going in the first car in about five minutes. You'll follow a minute or two later with your father.

FIONA. *(Nerves breaking)* Oh, I wish it was over! I wish it was over!

AUNT M. I know exactly how you feel. Like one of those astronauts waiting to be hurled into space and not knowing whether you're coming back or not.

FIONA. Don't talk like that, Auntie. You scare me.

PAULINE. *(Enters, crosses to sideboard, searching)* Nothing's going right. He's broken his cuff-link and he's in a terrible temper. There's one in here somewhere.

FIONA. Why does everyone have to leave everything till the last moment? I've been dressed for three hours.

PAULINE. It's easier for you, dear. You haven't got a husband to contend with. Oh, dear I can't find it. I'm sure we had one in a cracker last Christmas.

AUNT M. Couldn't he roll his sleeve up.

PAULINE. The coat's too small for that. *(Turning sees the untidy state of the room)* Oh, look at this room! And this morning I spent hours.

AUNT M. It only looks lived in, Pauline.

PAULINE. Yes, lived in by a tribe of savages. I can't have people back here with the place in this state. I shan't be able to go. I shall have to stay here and clear up.

HERBERT. *(Upstairs off, shouting)* Pauline, what the blazes are you doing down there?

PAULINE. *(Beside herself with frustration, goes to hall and calls up)* Be quiet, Herbert. I've got enough worries as it is.

JENNY. *(Enters Excitably)* There's quite a crowd gathered outside. You know, just like when the Police arrest someone and smuggle him away under a blanket.

PAULINE. *(Annoyed)* Your sister won't be under a blanket, Jenny.

FIONA. *(Nerves again)* I'm beginning to wish I was.

PAULINE. *(To JENNY)* You go out front and tell us as soon as the car comes.

JENNY. It's like in the French Revolution when the aristocrats were waiting for the tumbrils to arrive. *(She goes out.)*

AUNT M. She's getting so excited she'll be sick.

PAULINE. *(Finding a shoe)* Now, who left their shoe down here for everyone to fall over. Really! This family!

FIONA. They're yours, mother.

HERBERT. *(Storming in)* Well, I'm damned. Down here changing your shoes while I'm up there waiting for a cuff-link.

PAULINE. *(Almost screaming at him)* I can't find it. If you had sons you could rely on picking up a spare cuff-link when you wanted one.

FIONA. *(Bursting into tears)* You've always resented us girls, daddy, haven't you? That's why you've been so keen on getting us married off.

HERBERT. Oh, my God, don't you start.

AUNT M. She's a little on edge, Herbie. There, dear. *(She comforts FIONA.)*

PAULINE. I've simply got to clear this room up before I can go, Herbert.

HERBERT. You what?

PAULINE. If that Mrs. Dunjon walked into this room in this state she'd pass out.

HERBERT. Damned good idea, too. In any case, why worry about the room. We can keep them out in the tent. I'll have to tie this up with a bit of string or something. *(He goes out and hurries upstairs.)*

PAULINE. Melinda, is my slip showing.

AUNT M. It's showing more than your skirt. *(She adjusts PAULINE's skirt.)*

PAULINE. I dressed in such a hurry I'm not sure I've got everything on.

AUNT M. Don't worry. We're not likely to be searched.

JENNY. *(Appearing at doorway.)* Mummy, I feel sick. *(She runs off towards kitchen.)*

AUNT M. I thought that would happen.

PAULINE. *(Hurrying off to Kitchen)* Jenny, Jenny can't you leave it till we get back?

FIONA. I feel a bit sick, too.

AUNT M. Stand by the window and take a deep breath.

FIONA. *(Doing so)* Phew!

AUNT M. What is it?

FIONA. Those onions dad's got out there. They stink the place out.

AUNT M. Turn this way, then.

FIONA. *(Doing so, and taking a very deep breath)* Oh, no! Something's come away. *(She reaches behind to the small of her back.)* Oh, Auntie, is it all right?

AUNT M' *(Examing dress)* It's nothing. Just a stitch or two. You'd better stop breathing.

FIONA. What!

AUNT M. I don't mean altogether. I mean deep breathing Don't worry, it'll hold.

PAULINE. *(Entering in a flurry)* The car's here, Melinda. Are you ready?

HERBERT. *(Off; shouting)* The car's here, Pauline. Don't hang about now.

JENNY. *(Entering, very subdued)* Goodbye, Fiona.

PAULINE. You go and sit in the car and keep quiet.

JENNY. I wish it was an ambulance . *(She goes morosely out.)*

HERBERT. *(Appearing fully dressed with two rows of medals on his morning coat)* Come along now. Don't keep the chauffeur waiting.

JENNY. *(Reappearing)* There's a man to see you, Dad.

HERBERT. Where?

JENNY. At the front door. *(She goes)*

HERBERT. I hope they're not going to insist on payment for the cars now. *(He goes to the front door)*

FIONA. *(In a panic)* Where's my bouquet? I've lost my bouquet.

AUNT M. I put it in water in the kitchen. I'll get it. *(Goes out)*

PAULINE. Oh, darling, you look lovely. You know this is a day for a mother. It makes me look back over the years. Do you know I can remember when you were just a little eight-pound bundle.

FIONA. Can you, Mummy?

PAULINE. Yes, darling. I've got a good memory.

AUNT M. *(Entering with bouquet)* Here we are .... to complete the picture.

HERBERT. *(Enters from front)* You two get along.

PAULINE. *(Kissing Fiona)* This is your day, my darling, that you've waited for for so long.

HERBERT. That was dodger Weems at the door. He's just reported that the groom's at the church ... looking shell shocked. But he's there.

AUNT M. I'll try and sit at the end of the pew so I can give you confidence.

PAULINE. Oh, my baby, that this should happen to you.. at last!

JENNY. *(Appearing in doorway)* Come on. The driver wants to get away so he can watch the end of the Test Match. *(Goes out)*

AUNT M. *(Taking PAULINE's arm)* That's all men think about .... games. *(She goes out with PAULINE.)*

FIONA. Dad, you're not going to wear those medals, are you?

HERBERT. Of course. Formal occasion. You're expected to.

FIONA. *(Examining one of them)* The Victoria Cross. You never told me you'd won the Victoria Cross.

HERBERT. Didn't I? Well, I won so many. Can't be expected to remember them all. I want you to be proud of me today, Fiona, as I'm proud of you.

FIONA. Are you proud of me?

HERBERT. Of course. I know you didn't mean it when you said just now that I'd wanted to get you married off in a hurry.

FIONA. I spoke hastily. I'm sorry.

HERBERT. No one knows better than you the sacrifices I've made. Now that you're making a good marriage I daresay ... not immediately perhaps, but in the fullness of time.... you'll want to repay your old father.

FIONA. What do you mean?

HERBERT. Your Gerald is going to be a pretty wealthy man sooner or later. Those supermarkets make a packet. If nothing else, the occasional bottle of Scotch would make me feel I was not entirely forgotten by my favourite daughter

FIONA. *(Flinging herself into his arms)* Oh, Daddy, you have been good to me.

HERBERT. *(An arm about her, comforting her)* Now darling, don't cry.

FIONA. *(Between her sobs)* You're crying too. I can feel your tears.

HERBERT. *(Looking upward is hit in the eye by water dripping from the ceiling)* They're not tears. Some bloody fool's turned that cistern on. *(He dashes out)*

QUICK CURTAIN.

Scene Three. The same, about half-past four on the afternoon of the wedding. When the curtain rises the room is empty. The noise of a party comes from the marquee in the garden, talking, an occasional outburst of laughter, against the background of a radiogram playing pop music.

After a few moments PAULINE enters from the garden, closely followed by AUNT MELINDA.

PAULINE. *(Distraught and over-dramatic)* Oh, the mockery of it all, Melinda. The hollow mockery!

AUNT M. *(Trying to placate her)* Gerald was only arguing that they had a legal right to start their honeymoon today.

PAULINE. Poor wretched Fiona! Did you see her face as we left the church. And I suppose that organist thought it was funny playing us out to Chopin's Funeral March.

AUNT M. That wasn't the Funeral March, dear. I know it sounded like it.

PAULINE. And Herbert acting like a mad bull, threatening to sue the vicar. All in all a horrible fiasco!

AUNT M. It kept fine, though. Phew! it's stifling in here. *(She moves to hallway)* Do you mind if I open the front door to let some air through. *(PAULINE nods but AUNT M. has already gone into hall, to return almost immediately.)* Why don't you creep away upstairs and lie down for a while?

PAULINE. I won't lie down but I might take a couple of bottles of aspirin. ... to deaden the pain.

AUNT M. It's the anti-climax that's done it

PAULINE. *(On the verge of tears)* Humiliation, you mean. *(She goes out and upstairs).*

AUNT M. finds it very hot. Collapsing into arm-chair D. R. she takes off a shoe and fans her-self with it. IVY and RONALD enter from the garden. They don't see AUNT M. Her chair having its back towards them.

RONALD. I'm glad to get out of that tent. It was beginning to smell like a Turkish bordello.

IVY. *(Most severely)* And how would you know what a Turkish bordello smells like?

RONALD. *(Taken aback by her acid tone)* I don't, of course.

IVY. Then why say it?

RONALD. *(Lamely, excusing himself?)* Just one of my fancies!

IVY. *(More business-like)* I will agree that there is something indecent about this reception in the circumstances.

RONALD. I can see their point in carrying on with it. There won't be time in the morning if they're going to catch that plane.

IVY. *(Sitting L. end of settee)* I've heard of several weddings that have been postponed because the groom was missing and one or two because the bride was missing but when the wedding is postponed because the Vicar is missing ... well, that looks like Divine providence.

RONALD. Look, Ivy, we've done our duty and put in an appearance. What about slipping away quietly now?

IVY. And abandon Gerald to the mercies of that mob *(Indicating the direction of the marquee)* What sort of a mother do you think I am?

RONALD. But he is a married man, dear. Well ... almost.

IVY. Poor boy! Butchered to make a Farson's holiday! We just can't stand by and let this happen.

RONALD. *(Desperately)* But what can you do? It's no
use talking to him. I'm convinced that that fellow
Farson has got him under some sort of hypnosis.

IVY. Now that the wedding has been postponed time is
on our side. *(She rises)* I'm ready to make a move.
This evening we invite him for a last drink with us at
our hotel. He won't refuse his mother. A couple of
my sleeping pills are popped into his sherry. When
they begin to work we'll have Jackson take him out
and put him in the Daimler. Then we can all be on
the midnight flight to Bermuda.

RONALD. *(Buttering her up)* My, goodness Ivy, that's
brilliant.

IVY. Quite. And now I'm going to show myself in
that foetid tent. I may be a conspirator but I don't
like looking like one.

*She goes off into the garden, AUNT M. fanning
herself too vigorously with her shoe allows
it to slip out of her hand and fly across the room.
RONALD almost off, turns, sees show and then AUNT
M. arising from her chair D. R.*

RONALD. Did you throw that at me?

AUNT M. It slipped. *(She retrieves the shoe and puts it
on.)*

RONALD. You've been sitting there listening.

AUNT M. Couldn't help it, could I?

RONALD. *(With a snort)* This is a disgusting house.
(Turns to go)

AUNT M. Eh, you! Come back.

RONALD. What?

AUNT M. I thought I'd seen your face before ... and not
only your face.

RONALD. What are you talking about?

AUNT M. Barbizan Hotel, Bournemouth, Room 203.
Like a good detective I checked in my little book.
Do you know you were only my third case ?

RONALD. I'm sure I don't know what you're blithering about.

AUNT M. You were married at the time so you had to get a divorce in order to marry her *(Indicating direction of the garden)* ... and her money.

RONALD. This is slander.

AUNT M. It's only slander if I tell the others. Shall I do that? Then you can sue me.

JENNY. *(Entering from the garden)* It's stifling in that tent. They want more ice. They're even putting it in their tea. Having a good time. Mr. Dunjon ?*(She crosses R.)*

RONALD. Unbelievable.

JENNY. *(Brightly)* That's good. *(She goes out to kitchen).*

RONALD. Now listen to me. What game are you playing?

AUNT M. I want to improve you as a father-in-law.

RONALD. Ugh!

AUNT M. In the first place stop interfering with Fiona and Gerald. And you can drop this stunt your missus and you have cooked up to kidnap the lad. I'm not going to have Fiona disappointed again. It might be the undoing of her.

RONALD. I don't see why you imagine you can order me about.

AUNT M. I think you would if I played you the tape.

RONALD. Tape? What tape?

AUNT M. My boss always insisted on it with the new girls in the profession. And you were one of my earliest cases.

RONALD. Now you listen ....

AUNT M. No you listen. You'd had a few drinks that night. Your tongue was a bit free ... too free. Do you think Ivy would like to hear some of the callous things you said about her .... and why you were marrying her? It's all on the tape.

RONALD. *(Deflated and beaten after a pause, sinks into settee)* What have I got to do?

AUNT M. Be a bit nicer to Fiona. And talk your missus
into being a bit nicer to her, too. That's all. I shall
be keeping an eye on you from now on. 'Bye for now.
(She goes out to the garden).

PAULINE. *(Comes downstairs and enters).* Hello, there!
What's the matter? Pace a bit hectic for you?

RONALD. I was just turning things over.

PAULINE. Do you feel sick? You're not always so green
are you?

RONALD. I meant, turning over in my head.

PAULINE. Ah, nausea! Rotten, isn't it? I get it myself
sometimes. You're probably unbalanced, I mean, it's
a question of balance, you know. It's in the ear.

RONALD. Really!

FIONA. *(Enters from garden. She sweeps off her headress
and veil. It trails over RONALD's head)* Phew! It's hot.
(Seeing RONALD as he fights free of the veil) Oh!
hello, Mr. Dunjon. Having a good time?

RONALD. I've never enjoyed myself in quite the same
way.

PAULINE. I think you ought to get used to calling Mr.
Dunjon, father. Or Dad. Or Daddy, Or Popa, Or ....

RONALD. *(With a groan)* Anything but Pops, please.

PAULINE. Don't you think she looks lovely in white?

FIONA. It doesn't make me look washed out?

RONALD. Oh, no! You're a blooming bride if ever I
saw one.

FIONA. I'm so glad you approve of me. I was worried
in church. You were scowling. I really thought you
were going to be sick.

PAULINE. He suffers from nausea, dear.

FIONA. Oh! Poor Pops!

RONALD. I usually look like that when I'm ... very
happy.

FIONA. You're beginning to like me, aren't you? I must
give you a little kiss.

RONALD. *(Glancing towards garden)* Well, I don't know..

I suppose it will be all right.

FIONA. *(Leaning over him to kiss his cheek, she falls into his lap)* We're going to get along fine, Pops.

IVY. *Entering from the garden)* And what do you think you're doing, Ronald?

RONALD. *(Struggling up)* I ... I ... Well, she is our daughter-in-law, Ivy. Or will be.

IVY. No excuses, please. You know I disapprove of intimacy between relatives.

RONALD. Only too well.

IVY. *(Giving him a hard long look)* You must be drunk.

RONALD. Hardly likely, on one sherry in a glass that smelt of pickled onions.

AUNT M. *(Enters from garden)* I've been sent in to prepare for the cutting of the cake.

IVY. Ronald, I think we ought to be going.

FIONA. Oh, no Mums, you can't go till we've cut the cake.

IVY. I'm sure we can take that as read.

RONALD. I think we ought to do what Fiona wants. It is her day.

IVY. What! Ronald .. come here. I want to talk to you. *(She goes out into garden.)*

RONALD. *(Reluctantly following her)* Excuse me, please.

AUNT M. *(As he passes her)* Keep it up. You're doing all right.

FIONA. Well, I want to freshen up a bit before the ceremonials. *(She goes out and upstairs)*

PAULINE. *(As a roar comes from the marquee)* Are they still arguing out there?

AUNT M. Perhaps you'd better come out with me and calm them down a bit.

PAULINE. *(Tearfully)* I don't know. It's not like an ordinary wedding. *(She and AUNT M. go out to garden.)*

JOHNNY. *(Enters, alone for a moment, looks about him, then JENNY enters from kitchen with jug of ice cubes).*

Jenny!

JENNY. Oh, you've come back.

JOHNNY. I'm sorry I missed your wedding. How did everything go off?

JENNY. Oh, lovely!

JOHNNY. So you're Mrs..Modigliani now.

JENNY. *(Mystified)* Am I? *(Pause: looks at him with agitation)* I don't know whether you ought to stay or not.

JOHNNY. You're not turning me out, are you?

JENNY. No. But you're going to get an awful surprise if you stay.

JOHNNY. I can't go yet. I've got to clear up this mystery of Fiona.

JENNY. Is there a mystery?

JOHNNY. I've been looking for her in Leatherhead. I didn't find the hospital. I asked at the Police Station They told me I was the one who ought to be inside.

JENNY. I can't lie to you, Johnny. She's here. I'll....... *(Moving to doorway)* I'll get her. *(Hesitates)* But you must be prepared for a shock. She's... well, she's different. *(She goes out and calls from foot of stairs.)* Fiona, someone to see you. A man.

JOHNNY. *(As Jenny returns to room)* I can never forgive myself for what I've done to her.

JENNY. Johnny ... when she comes in she'll be ... she'll be wearing a wedding dress.

JOHNNY. You mean ... she still wears it ... since last March. Oh, how terrible! Poor girl!

JENNY. *(Not knowing how to cope further)* It's Miss Havisham all over again.

FIONA. *(Appearing in doorway)* Who is it?

JOHNNY. Hello, Fido!

FIONA. Johnny.

JOHNNY. Poor Fiona! *(Goes to embrace her)* But don't worry. I'll get you well again.

FIONA. I feel better already.

JOHNNY *(Surprised)* Really!

FIONA. *(Pushing him away from her)* Eh, just a minute. Why didn't you turn up for our wedding?

JOHNNY. That's what I've come to tell you.

JENNY. *(Moving towards french windows)* I'll try and keep the hordes at bay for a few minutes.

FIONA. There's a dear. Do a strip tease out there if necessary.

JENNY. That won't be all that novel. Dad's already got his shirt off. *(She goes out to garden.)*

JOHNNY. *(Embracing FIONA again)* Darling, Fido. I've waited so long.

FIONA. *(Pushing him away)* I'm afraid you've waited too long ... six months too long.

JOHNNY. I couldn't help letting you down. Believe me.

FIONA. Humiliating me, you mean. Do you know what it's like standing at the church door and listening to *Here Comes The Bride played seventeen times?*

JOHNNY. You'd get to know it, I suppose.

FIONA. *(Stamping her foot angrily)* I didn't go to St. George's for a music lesson, Johnny.

JOHNNY. *(Breaking L. desperately trying to explain)* Look, the postal strike was on. I couldn't write or telegraph. You haven't got a phone. I did the only thing I could think of. I phoned the vicar and asked him to explain as tactfully as he could.

FIONA. He said something about you being detained. I thought he meant a couple of minutes. Not six months.

JOHNNY. That was the trouble. It was six months. Now, don't be angry with me. I did it all for you. I wanted to be worthy of you.

FIONA. Funny way to show it.

JOHNNY. You know that when we planned to get married I only had about twenty pounds in the whole world. But I wanted to give you all the nice things a girl expects.

FIONA. *(Acidly)* Like being left at the altar rail!

JOHNNY. No, listen, Fiona. You know I went up to see my folks about a fortnight before the wedding.

FIONA. I did expect you to come back.

JOHNNY. So did I. Especially when I had that phenomenal lucky run on the dogs ... due to the fact that my old man knew which ones were doped. I turned that twenty pounds into two hundred. Then, one evening, I went up West to one of those casino places. I'll turn this two hundred into two thousand I said.

FIONA. Don't tell me. You lost the lot.

JOHNNY. And a bit besides. Well, then I got talked into it, you see. This job ... they said it was easy.

FIONA. Now I know where all your lovely hair's gone. You've been in prison.

JOHNNY. Six months. First offence. I ought to have got off. I had one of these psychiatric chaps talking to me. Told the court all my shortcomings as a citizen were due to the way my old man had bashed me about when I was a kid. Very convincing. Well, he must have been. Next day they had my old man up and fined him fifty nicker for cruelty to children. But it didn't do me any good.

FIONA. Oh, Johnny. It's all too late now. I would have waited ....

HERBERT. *(Entering from garden)* Oh, you're back.

JOHNNY. You sent me on a wild goose chase, Mr. Farso

HERBERT. Look boy, You had your chance last March. Now it's someone else's turn.

JOHNNY. *(Turning to FIONA)* You've been married this afternoon while I was in Leatherhead.

JENNY. *(Entering from garden)* Looks like a storm brewing up.

FIONA. Oh, darling, I can't explain. It's too awful.

JENNY. Aye, aye. *Wuthering Heights all over* again!

PAULINE. *(Entering from garden with AUNT M.)* You shouldn't be here.

HERBERT. *(Grandly)* He's here on suffrance. Pauline. He'll cause no trouble.

RONALD, IVY and GERALD enter from garden.

IVY. Gerald isn't too well. I think it would be a good idea if he came with us to the hotel and lay down for an hour or two.

HERBERT. If he needs laying down, I'll do it. Now, where are the others?

PAULINE. They said to carry on without them. They're quite happy out there. *(Indicates direction of Marquee)*

FIONA. *(Takes Johnny's hand and leads him D.C. towards GERALD)* Oh, Johnny, you haven't met Gerald, have you? Gerald is going to be my husband. *(She doesn't sound overjoyed)*

JOHNNY. I don't understand what's going on.

HERBERT. You don't have to understand. *(Bellowing)* Sit down.

Scared by his voice, GERALD, FIONA and JOHNNY sit on settee in one movement. FIONA is in the centre.

HERBERT. Now, let's get some order into these proceedings. Telegrams first. Where's that best man of yours got to?

GERALD. Peter? He went home. He wasn't feeling too well.

HERBERT' Ten minutes ago he was guzzling my pickled onions.

GERALD. That's why he doesn't feel well.

HERBERT. Namby, pamby! Well, you'd better read them, then, Melinda. You're natural. *(Hands telegrams to Melinda.)*

VICAR *(Entering from hall)* Ah, dearly beloved brethren, I see we are all gathered. Ah, there you are, Miss Fiona. I've been chasing all over Surrey for you and you're going to tell me you've been here all the time.

FIONA. *(Testily)* Not all the time, Vicar. I did spend a half-hour at your church.

VICAR. *(Turning to JOHNNY)* You're Mr. Spinet, aren't you? It was you who rang me. *(Wagging an admonitory finger at him.)* I don't think it was very funny, young man.

FIONA. Don't blame him, Vicar.

JOHNNY. It was Mr. Farson who told me Fiona had gone crazy.

IVY. *(To RONALD)* Well he ought to know.

HERBERT. No need for any fuss. We're just doing things in a different order, that's all. There's nothing in the law that says you can't have the reception before the wedding.

VICAR. Ah, that's wonderful. There'll be a happy ending after all, Miss Fiona, you'll see.

FIONA. *(Making sheep's eyes at JOHNNY who looks very mournful)* I'm not so sure now. *(Stifles a sob.)*

AUNT M. I'll make a start on the telegrams.

JOHNNY. I don't think I want to hear them. *(He begins to rise)*

FIONA. No, don't go yet, Johnny.

HERBERT. *(Pushing JOHNNY back into his seat)* You stay where you are. It won't do you any harm to witness this young man's happiness. *(Indicating GERALD who looks pretty miserable)* It'll haunt you for the rest of your days.

FIONA. I don't want him haunted for the rest of his days.

AUNT M. The first one is from Sidney Meisterman.

HERBERT. Old Sid, eh! He used to be my partner in the days when we ran the book. What's he say?

AUNT M. He says, 'Congratulations. May all your troubles be little ones.'

HERBERT. *(Guffawing)* May all your troubles be little ones.' That's real witty. He always was a wag.

FIONA. *(Whimpering)* I don't want my troubles to be little ones.

GERALD. There, there, darling. They soon grow up.

FIONA. I don't want them to be big ones either.

IVY. I really don't think it proper to discuss the size of the family when the wedding has not yet taken place.

JENNY. *(Picking up her camera from sideboard)* Can I take a picture now? Just for the record, as they say.

AUNT M. Good idea. Come on, Ronald. A nice broad grin.

RONALD is able to do this now as he has been steadily drinking from a bottle of sherry ever since he came in from the garden.

IVY. Did you call my husband, Ronald?

AUNT M. Why not? You get friendly at weddings.

IVY. I don't know that I do.

RONALD. You don't get friendly anywhere.

IVY. *(Most severely)* Ronald, I will not tolerate tawdy balk. I mean, bawdy talk.

RONALD. Good Lord, that wasn't tawdy balk.

IVY. I'll be the judge of that.

PAULINE. I should leave the photography till later, dear. When everyone's more relaxed. *(Rather reluctantly JENNY obeys, putting the camera back on the sideboard.)* Who's the next telegram from, Melinda?

AUNT M. The next one is from Granny and Grumps Pipkiss.

HERBERT. Never heard of them.

PAULINE. Oh, Herbert! That's my mother and father.

HERBERT. No? I thought they died about ten years ago.

PAULINE. That shows how much interest you take in me. I've often told you that I keep in touch with them.

HERBERT. I thought you meant through the ouija board.

PAULINE. Ugh! What have they got to say?

AUNT M. 'Congratulations. May all your troubles be little ones.'

HERBERT. Bloody original old couple, I must say.

GERALD. *(Still trying to console FIONA)* We won't have any little ones, not for a while, if you don't want any.

FIONA. *(Casting eyes at JOHNNY)* It's not that.

AUNT M. This one's from Sister Teresa.

VICAR. Sister Teresa from the Convent of the Scared Heart. What a very nice gesture!

PAULINE. No, Vicar, Fiona's sister Teresa. I've told you about her. She's the one that can't have any children. There's something wrong with her husband's genes.

VICAR. *(Not quite understanding)* Too tight?

PAULINE. Oh, no, he's quite generous.

VICAR. I'm afraid I don't follow.

PAULINE. Oh, I don't mean the jeans you wear, Vicar.

VICAR. I never wear them.

PAULINE. No, but some people do.

VICAR. That's true.

PAULINE. Well, I'm not talking about them.

VICAR. Oh!

PAULINE. No, I was talking about what makes you a boy or a girl.

VICAR. Really, Mrs. Farson, I thought most people knew that.

PAULINE. Yes, but it all depends on your father.

VICAR. *(After a while)* Do you know I never quite understood that before. Thank you for making it so clear to me.

AUNT M. Anyway, Sister Teresa says: 'Congratulations. May all your ...

Everyone joins in the chorus: Troubles be little ones.'

IVY. *(Contemptuously)* They must have run them off on duplicating machine.

AUNT M. One more. *(Reading)* 'This is to warn you that unless your Gas account is paid within seven days the Board will .....

HERBERT. *(Snatching the letter from her)* Don't read that out. Obviously delivered here by mistake.

AUNT M. That's the lot, then.

IVY. Thank goodness for that. I hate sentiment.

RONALD. Why don't you have a nice drink of Prussic Acid .... and enjoy yourself.

IVY. Ronald ! I'm going to have a severe talk with you when I get you home.

RONALD. *(Grinning tipsily at her)* In that case, I'm not coming.

IVY. What makes you think you've got a choice.

DEREK. *(Entering from hall)* Sorry to intrude. Front door was open.

HERBERT. *(Bellowing)* You again!

JENNY. Oh, Derek, come in. Don't be scared.

HERBERT. What do you want? Can't you see that this is an intimate family occasion?

DEREK. Strictly business, Mr. Farson. And business that can't wait.

HERBERT. My daughter's got no business with you.

JENNY. Oh, yes, I have.

HERBERT. I've warned you before. Now get out of here, you white slaver, before I flay you alive.

JENNY. If you touch him, Daddy, I shall leave home.

PAULINE. Oh, Jenny .... no .... *(To HERBERT)* If you drive her to that ... I'll

DEREK. I want you to leave home in any case. Paris for you, my girl. That's where we've decided to make it.

JENNY. Paris! Oh, how marvellous! *(She hugs him)*

DEREK. *(Noticing HERBERT, aghast and speechless)* Oh, it's quite all right. She'll be under contract. Here. Look. *(He thrusts the contract into HERBERT's hands)*

HERBERT. I don't want to look at that. What's it for, anyway. Dancing in some joint in Istanbul? Well, that's what I think of your contract. *(He tears it up.)*

JENNY. *(In tears)* Oh, Daddy, you've ruined my life.

DEREK. If you don't really want your daughter to earn two hundred a month ... and better things to come ..

HERBERT. Two hundred a month? Two hundred pour do you mean?

DEREK. Just for a start. I daresay it'll be a good deal m by the end of the year.

PAULINE. Oh, Herbert, what have you done?

HERBERT. *(Dropping to his knees and collecting the pieces of the torn contract.)* Don't panic, woman. Just find the selotape quickly.

DEREK. Oh, don't bother. I've got another copy. You' have to okay it, Mr. Farson. And of course because Jenny's a minor you'll be holding the money in trust for her.

HERBERT. *(Brightening)* Will I? Oh, yes, of course. Ye of course, I'll do that. Only too pleased. I always said she was the cleverest one in the family, didn't I, Pauline? *(Shaking hands with DEREK)* It's certainly nice to meet you, Mr. Colbert.

DEREK. How do you do?

HERBERT. Now that you're here, Mr. Colbert, I hope you'll take a glass of champers with us.

DEREK. Very kind of you. But I've only got a few minutes. I want your permission to take Jenny off your hands for the evening.

HERBERT. Certainly my dear Derek. Anything you say

DEREK. J.A. wants to meet her. He's at the Hilton. He wants us to go up this evening and have dinner with I

HERBERT. Our little festivities are almost at an end. Melinda give out the glasses. I'm coming round with champagne.

AUNT M. takes round glasses on a tray and HERBERT follows pouring the champagne.

VICAR. This is indeed a happy moment. Out of the jaws of defeat cometh forth sweetness.

PAULINE. Vicar, you do have a lovely way of putting things.

VICAR. I needed all my skill with words in Leatherhead a couple of hours ago.

FIONA. Why were you in Leatherhead when you ought to have been at St. George's?

JOHNNY. I rang him from Leatherhead. It was the only thing I could think of doing when I couldn't find the hospital.

VICAR. And I ... I was intent on hurrying to your bedside. But I couldn't find the hospital, either. I asked at the police station. They thought it was some stunt for Rag Week. Someone had already been asking before me. I had to do some fast talking, I can tell you.

HERBERT. Never mind. What about you, dear? *(To IVY)*

IVY. The teeniest drop. I'm allergic to anything but Napoleon brandy. *(HERBERT makes sure she has the 'teeniest drop')*

JENNY. Derek, what did you mean this morning when you said that no woman could put up with your obsession?

PAULINE. Obsession? What's that? Who's got an obsession?

HERBERT. Oh, don't fuss, mother. Clever people like that are entitled to be a bit queer.

PAULINE. I don't want him being queer with my daughter.

DEREK. I meant my obsession with film-making. That's all I think about.

JENNY. *(Disappointed)* All?

DEREK. Yes, night and day. All my wives have had the same complaint.

HERBERT. How intolerant of them Derek old boy!

DEREK. I can't blame them. No woman likes to play second fiddle to a Leica.

GERALD. This is jolly good champagne.

AUNT M. You're not supposed to be drinking it yet.

IVY. Oh, let the boy enjoy himself while he still can.

JOHNNY. I want to warn you, brother. You'd better treat Fiona okay. Otherwise you'll have me to deal with.

PAULINE. Now, don't you two boys quarrel over Fio Not on her wedding day. Or even the day before.

HERBERT. Right, I think everyone's topped up. Well, Pauline, you were on the stage once. I reckon you'r the one to put passion into this.

PAULINE. I haven't put passion into anything for yea *(Pause)* It's all a bit too much for me. My eldest daughter ... married at last.

FIONA. *(A sharp rebuke)* No need for the 'at last', mother.

VICAR. Just a minute. I haven't got any.

HERBERT. You must have drunk it.

VICAR. I would have known that, surely.

HERBERT. I distinctly remember splashing some dow your ...

PAULINE. Oh, don't argue, Herbert. You can share m Vicar.

HERBERT. Right, then. Now, everyone raise your gla

PAULINE. You said I was doing this.

HERBERT. Well, get on this it, then.

PAULINE. I give you a toast. Ladies and gentlemen ... Oh, no. I can't do it. It's asking too much of a moth

She breaks down. The VICAR comforts her.

DEREK. I wish they'd get on with it. I want to get yo up to the Hilton. And, before we go, for goodness sa do something to your hair.

JENNY. *(Offended)* What's wrong with my hair?

DEREK. It looks so tatty. Haven't you got a wig?

JENNY. *(Sharply)* No, I have not got a wig.

DEREK. Don't speak to me like that, Jenny. I'm your employer now and I've got to sell you to J.A., remember.

GERALD. I haven't got any champagne.

FIONA. You drank it. And mine.

AUNT M. You don't want champagne anyway. Really they ought to be cutting the cake.

HERBERT. You're quite right. Come on Gerald.

GERALD rises and helps HERBERT to move the table bearing the cake to D.C. JOHNNY takes the chance to press FIONA's hand.

GERALD. It's pretty heavy.

IVY. He shouldn't be using up his strength that way. He ought to have a best man to do it for him.

GERALD. Come on Fiona. *(FIONA rises and comes to table)* You pick up the knife. I put my hands on top of yours. Now, at the given word, lunge.

FIONA. What's the given word?

GERALD. I don't know. I'll give you a nudge.

IVY. I think I'm going to pass out. I've come over quite numb.

AUNT M. That's circulation trouble. Get your hubby to give you a nice rub when you get to bed tonight.

RONALD. *(Brightening ... slightly tipsy)* That's a good idea.

IVY. You'll do nothing of the sort. I forbid you even to think about it.

HERBERT. Oh, come on, you two. Get that blessed cake cut.

FIONA. He hasn't given me the nudge yet.

HERBERT. For God's sake, then, give her the nudge, and let's get on.

GERALD. *(Giving her a nudge)* All right. Here we go. *(Great effort is put into piercing the icing of the cake but to no avail.)* Let's come down from a more acute angle. *(They do so without success.)*

FIONA. What did you make this with, Jenny? Plaster of Paris?

JENNY. It's Royal icing. It's inclined to be a bit hard.

GERALD. Are you pulling or pushing?

FIONA. I'm straining every muscle I've got.

One last desperate effort results in the "trick" knife

bending into an ellipse.

GERALD. Oh, I say!

PAULINE. Oh, look what you've done. My best knife.

HERBERT. *(Guffawing)* Shall I get my hacksaw?

FIONA. Oh, never mind the cake.

HERBERT. That's right. We can work on that later whe
we've got more time.

PAULINE. Ladies and Gentlemen, I give you the bride
groom.

VICAR. No, wait a minute. You can't say that, you kno

IVY. Of course you can't. You can say prospective or
potential or possible or some such term.

HERBERT. Oh, don't quibble. To Fiona and Gerald. M
they always be as happy as they are at this moment.

*GERALD stretches out his arms to take
FIONA. She stares at him. Tears in her eyes.
JOHNNY rises from the settee and is standing to her L. She turns, looks at him and
flings herself into JOHNNY's arms. A warm
embrace. FIONA is sobbing with relief.*

GERALD. I say, I'm here. *(He taps FIONA on the
shoulder)*

PAULINE. Fiona, what are you doing? Oh, the mocker
The mockery!

GERALD. That's hardly the way to carry on, Fiona. I
feel such a fool standing here.

IVY. Now I've seen it with my own eyes. Adultery
before they're even married.

RONALD. *(Feeling, under AUNT M. eyes that he must
take a lenient view of FIONA's conduct)* Not to wor
I think it was a genuine mistake.

HERBERT. Pull yourself together, Fiona. You're
behaving as though he was the best man.

FIONA. *(Breaking away from the embrace and facing
the company defiantly)* He is the best man, too. The
best man I've ever know in my life.

There is a stunned silence for a few moments.

GERALD. *(At last)* Fiona, what about me? Where do I
    fit in?

FIONA. *(Compassionately)* Oh, you're a darling, Gerald.

IVY. He's not. He's a fool. I've said so all along.

JOHNNY. It's perfectly simple. I love Fiona and Fiona
    loves me.

HERBERT. You have the gall to stand there and say
    that at the very moment we are drinking the health of
    the bride and groom.

JOHNNY. Better late then never.

IVY. *(Rising)* Of course, this completely alters the
    situation. I am withdrawing my boy from the wedding.

HERBERT. What do you mean, withdrawing him? He's
    not a blooming racehorse.

VICAR. I wonder if I could say something which might
    clarify the matter.

PAULINE. *(Pleadingly)* No, Vicar, I don't think you
    could.

VICAR. Is the wedding still on for the morrow? That's
    all I want to know.

HERBERT.	IVY.
PAULINE. Yes, of course.	FIONA. No, of course not.
RONALD.	JOHNNY.
AUNT M.	

VICAR. I'm glad that's cleared up then.

GERALD. I'd like to know where I stand.

RONALD. *(Loud)* Sit down. *(GERALD obeys. Sits
    settee.)*

IVY. Don't talk to my son like that, Ronald.

GERALD. Fiona, think about me a bit.

FIONA. I'm sorry, Gerald. But life is like that, isn't it?

GERALD. But don't you care if I'm terriby upset.

FIONA. I don't think you are.

DEREK. I can't hang about any longer, Jenny. I've got
    to get you up to see J.A. So come along

JENNY. I don't think I want to come.

DEREK. What?

JENNY. I've just realised how you think you own me ..
to be ordered about, placed in one of your sets as if I
were no more than a Dresden figure or a Chippendale
chair.

DEREK. I'm prepared to give you a decent contract. W
more can I do?

JENNY. I'd have put up with the ordering about if you
cared for me a bit as a woman. But you don't. I'm no
more than a piece of property to you ... and I'm not
going to put up with it. Not when I feel about you as
I do.

DEREK. You're turning down my offer.

JENNY. *(Quietly but firmly)* Yes.

DEREK. *(After staring at her, realising that she won't
change her mind)* I'm damned sorry it turned out like
this. I wanted you for that part. But that was all.

JENNY. Goodbye, Derek.

DEREK. There couldn't be anything else. My divorce h
come through. I'm getting married again next Wedne
For the fifth time! Poor woman! *(He goes out.)*

HERBERT. Oh, God, I can hardly believe it. A daughte
mine turning down two hundred a month.

PAULINE. *(Anxiously as JENNY moves towards door*
Where are you going, my darling?

JENNY. To my room. To re-read *How to attract
Men* . To find out where I went wrong. *(She goes ou
and upstairs.)*

IVY. I don't think there's any point in our staying any
longer, Ronald.

GERALD. Is the reception over, then?

HERBERT. The reception might be. But I'm holding yo
the promise to marry my daughter.

GERALD. She doesn't seem all that keen, Mr. Farson.

HERBERT. Ah, you've got to get used to women being
a bit ... highly-strung. This little charade doesn't mea
anything, son. Nerves, that's all.

GERALD. I'm trying to ignore it but ...

HERBERT. This other chap's so unreliable.

FIONA. Oh, father, stop trying to run other people's lives.

IVY. I don't know if you realise it, Mr. Farson but it is quite possible for the aggrieved groom to sue for breach of promise.

HERBERT. *(Alarmed)* No, you wouldn't do that.

IVY. *(Crossing to R.C.)* I shall consult my solicitors. Obviously my son has suffered a great deal, mentally and physically.

GERALD. *(With a politely lecherous glance at FIONA)* I wouldn't say I'd suffered physic ... *(The last syllable is lot in a screech of pain and GERALD is seized by cramp in the leg.)*

IVY. Miss Farson, did you stick something into him?

GERALD. *(In agony)* It's my leg. The muscle. Stiff as iron.

HERBERT. Oh, God, here he goes again.

PAULINE. Oh, Herbert, the poor boy's in pain.

IVY. *(Up to doorway)* Are you coming or aren't you?

GERALD. *(Grimacing and bouncing about on his stiff leg)* Of course, I'm coming.

IVY. Then why are you going in the opposite direction?

GERALD. *(Whose painful leg has carried him D.L.)* I have no control over myself, mother.

IVY. I can quite believe that. It's been your trouble all along. Now come on. *(SHE sweeps out.)*

GERALD. *(At last able to move himself in the direction of the doorway)* Goodbye, everyone. *(To FIONA and JOHNNY)* And may all your troubles be little ones! *(He goes out)*

RONALD. *(Rising tipsily from his seat U.L.)* I won't say too much. On the whole it's been a successful day. Thank you Vicar, for what you didn't do.

VICAR. Oh, it was nothing. Nothing.

RONALD. That's what I mean. *(To AUNT M.)* I wonder if we shall meet a third time.

AUNT M. I doubt it. I detest men.

RONALD. That'd be a fifty per cent improvement on
Ivy. She detests men ... and women. Goodbye all. *(He
goes out.)*

VICAR. Well, I thought it was a very nice reception. Eve
one acted perfectly. And that reminds me what it wa
that brought me over here this morning.

PAULINE. Oh!

VICAR. Acting perfectly. It's a bit of a 'thing' with me,
you know. I want to get everything right, Now, in the
script it says, 'He gets down on his knees' and then
later, 'springing up.' I have to confess, Pauline, that m
sprinting days are over and I was wondering if ...

PAULINE. You called me Pauline.

VICAR. Did I?

PAULINE. Yes, you did ... Humphrey.

VICAR. Would you like to go over that part with me ...
to put my mind at rest? I was thinking that if I don't
go down so far I won't have so far to come up.

PAULINE. That's true. When do you want to try it?

VICAR. What about this evening? What about now? I
could run you over in my car and we could use the
settee in my den.

PAULINE. Why not? *(To HERBERT)* Cheerio! *(In the
doorway)* Why not get Mrs. Tovey to come in and giv
you a hand with the clearing up? *(She and the VICAI
go off)*

HERBERT. Well, I'm damned. I knew I never should ha
let her start with this dramatic business again. The
stage corrupts her so.

AUNT M. *(To FIONA and JOHNNY who are locked ir
an embrace on the settee)* What about you two?

FIONA. Oh, we're all right.

HERBERT. Now look here, young man. I've had enougl
trouble with you before. What are your intentions
towards my daughter this time, I'd like to know.

JOHNNY. Well, you can mind your own business. Fiona
and I are in love. If and when we decide to get married
is our business not yours.

HERBERT. It's me who has to pay for all the receptions.

FIONA. We'll give you plenty of notice, Dad. *(Rising)*
Now Johnny, where are you taking me?

JOHNNY. Anywhere you like, love.

FIONA. What! Dressed like this?

JOHNNY. All the better. You make a smashing bride.
(Arms about each other, they go out.)

HERBERT. *(Grumbling)* She's had enough practice at it.

AUNT M. Things did not turn out exactly as you planned,
Herbie.

HERBERT. Sometimes I don't think it's worth trying,
Melinda. The more you do for some people the less
grateful they are.

*HERBERT, Morose and defeated, sinks onto
settee.*

AUNT M. Oh, come on, Herbert dear. You're not the sort
to let things get you down. *(An idea suddenly strikes
her)* Oh, I've just remembered. I must get a picture.
(She dashes out into the hall.)

HERBERT. *(Calling after her)* What do you want a
picture of this shambles for?

AUNT M. *(Returning with a small camera)* A souvenir,
Something to remember.

HERBERT. I just want to forget.

AUNT M. Now, yes. But in years to come you'll have a
good laugh over this. Now come on, smile!

HERBERT. Oh, this is wet.

AUNT M. I've got a new reel in here. Colour! Come on,
watch the birdie!

HERBERT. I don't feel like smiling, Melinda.

AUNT M. Just a little one. You can turn it off as soon as
I've clicked.

*HERBERT makes an atrocious attempt to
smile.*

Oh, Herbert, you can do better than that. Look over your shoulder towards the wedding cake. *(HERBERT does as he's told. A look of exquisite agony comes on his face.)* That's better. *(HERBERT's lips are parted, his teeth gritted.)* Lovely! Now hold it for a moment. *(HERBERT, his right leg stiff, pushes himself out of the settee and dances awkwardly about the room while MELINDA tries to aim her camera.)*

Oh! please! Please, don't mess about Herbert.

HERBERT. I'm not messing about. I've got the bloody cramp.

As he jerks himself about the room and MELINDA tries to get her picture.....

THE CURTAIN FALLS

FURNITURE AND PROPERTIES PLOT

ACT ONE Scene 1 On stage:	Three piece suite, Two upright chairs, Sideboard with bottles and decanter and glasses on it, Small table, Standard lamp, Cushions, Pictures, Newspapers, etc. Carpets, rugs. Heavy curtains at french windows hung behind pelmet. Vases, flowers Mirror on wall above sideboard. Rose bowl. Needle and cotton in sideboard drawer.
Off stage:	Rose bowl, filled with roses, including 'Chastity' (Pauline). Bunch of roses for Herbert. Aerosol of laquer (Jenny) Secateurs (Herbert)
Personal:	False eyelashes (Jenny) Handkerchief (Herbert)
ACT ONE Scene 2 On stage:	As in previous scene
Off stage:	First aid tin containing, plasters, bandages, scissors, etc. Small bowel with water in it. Towel Wedding-dress.
Personal:	Watch (Derek).

ACT TWO	As in Act One with the addition of
Scene 1	postcards (Wedding congratulatory) on
On Stage:	mantel shelf and sideboard. Wedding
	cake and trick knife on small table
	U.L. Bits of clothing scattered on chairs
	and settee. Presents in various places,
	most still wrapped. An untidy general
	appearance. A bottle of champagne
	on sideboard. More glasses on sideboard.

Off stage:	Toast rack (wrapped for Jenny
	Morning suit (in box) for Jenny
	Carmen Miranda Hat (Aunt Melinda)
	Telegram (Jenny)

Personal:	Hair curlers,
	hair net,
	dressing-gown (Fiona)

ACT TWO	Pauline's shoes, in addition to
Scene 2. On stage:	above

Personal:	Two rows of medals on morning coat
	(Herbert)

ACT TWO	As Act Two, Scene 1, with the addition
Scene 3	of two or three empty bottles, telegrams
On stage:	on small table by cake. Jenny's camera
	on sideboard.

Personal:	Head-dress and veil (Fiona)
	Bottle of sherry (Ronald)
	Contract (Derek)

Off stage:	Camera (Aunt Melinda)

LIGHTING PLOT

Fittings required:

In Living room;
pendant
wall lights,
standard lamp,
In hall: Pendant

**Apparent sources
of light:**

By day:
Light from the french windows in
living-room.
Light through glass of front door
into hall.

To Open:

Effect of bright sunshine from
garden through french windows and
sunshine through front door into
hall. Could be faded slowly as
scene progresses.

Scene 2.

Right: Open in darkness.
Cue: Front door is opened. ON light
in hall.
Cue: As Jenny enters living-room she
switches on all lights either from one
switch or, preferably, first pendant,
then side-lights, then standard lamp.
No further cues.

**ACT TWO.
Scene One**

Morning sunlight from garden and
front door.
No cues.

Scene 2.

As above. No cues.

Scene 3.

Afternoon sunlight.
No cues.

REHEARSAL DATES

CAST NOTES